X-PLANES
at EDWARDS

Steve Pace

MBI Publishing Company

In memory of Lt. Gen. Laurence C. "Bill" Craigie, US Air Force (Retired), 1902–1994.
General Craigie, the first US military pilot to fly a jet-powered airplane, is also credited with overseeing the
development of six bombers, eleven fighters, two transports, and two trainers. General Craigie, a veteran of World War II and
the Korean War, died 27 February of natural causes. He was ninety-two.

Acknowledgments

Sincere thanks to: Mrs. Joyce A Baker, Mrs. Cheryl A Gumm, Dr. James O. Young, AFFTC/HO; Col. Joe Cotton, USAF (Ret.); Harry Gann, McDonnell Douglas Corporation; Lt. Col. Fitz Fulton, USAF (Ret.); Tony Landis; Douglas C. Nelson, AFFTC Museum; Don Nolan, NASA DFRF Public Affairs; Eric Schulzinger, Lockheed Corporation; Chris Wamsley; Greg Field, Zack Miller, Michael Haenggi, and the rest of the editorial staff at MBI Publishing.

First published in 1995 by MBI Publishing Company, PO Box 1, 729 Prospect Avenue, Osceola, WI 54020-0001 USA

TL567.R47P33   1995
629.13′072073—dc20   95-6121

The information in this book is true and complete to the best of our knowledge. All recommendations are made without any guarantee on the part of the author or Publisher, who also disclaim any liability incurred in connection with the use of this data or specific details.

We recognize that some words, model names and designations, for example, mentioned herein are the property of the trademark holder. We use them for identification purposes only. This is not an official publication.

MBI Publishing Company books are also available at discounts in bulk quantity for industrial or sales-promotional use. For details write to Special Sales Manager at Motorbooks International Wholesalers & Distributors, 729 Prospect Avenue, PO Box 1, Osceola, WI 54020-0001 USA.

Library of Congress Cataloging-in-Publication Data
Pace, Steve.
     X-planes at Edwards / Steve Pace.
        p.   cm. -- (Enthusiastic color series)
     Includes index.
        ISBN 0-87938-985-0 (pbk.)
        1. Research aircraft--California--Edwards Air Force
Base--History.   2. Airplanes--California--Edwards Air
Force Base--Flight testing--History.   I. Title.   II. Series.

On the front cover: The Grumman X-29—using its super-critical Forward Swept Wing (FSW), close-coupled canards, and flaps fitted to the rear strakes—executes a high angle of attack maneuver. Its fly-by-wire flight control system is triple redundant, using a three-channel digital system and an analog computer back up to minimize the chance of failure during flight. *NASA*

On the frontispiece page: As a North American B-25 Mitchell flies a practice low-level gun strafing run across her bow, the full-scale wooden model of a 650ft-long Mogami-class Japanese heavy cruiser, christened the *Muroc Maru*, sails across the western edge of the dry lake at Edwards AFB, circa 1944. *Rockwell*

On the title page: From high above, the Edwards AFB complex appears diminutive. Yet, at 301,000sq-ac, with 44sq-mi of useable landing area on Rogers and Rosamond Dry Lakes (including a main concrete runway length of 15,000ft), it is onw of the world's largest aircraft flight-test facilities. It would literally take days to hike around its perimeter. This view, captured in March 1991, shows a rare combination of water over parts of the lake and dust clouds from high winds. *USAF via AFFTC/HO*

On the back cover: The Northrop B-2A Advanced Technology Bomber is the first heavy bomber designed with stealth as its major design goal. A design once thrown away by the US Air Force because it was too radical, the flying-wing shape was resurrected after more than forty years because it was the ideal shape to help elude detection by radar. *Northrop*

Printed in Hong Kong

Contents

Introduction

Birds have been flying since prehistoric time, when pterodactyls roamed the skies above a much younger Earth. The human race did not match that extinct flying reptile's accomplishment until 1903, when mankind itself began to fly.

In our never-ending quest to discover better and safer ways to fly, mankind must continue to improve upon the four major disciplines associated with manned flight: aeronautics on the whole, aerodynamics, airframes, and powerplants.

Indeed, mankind has learned a great deal about flight in a relatively short period of time. In a little less than 100 years, we have learned how to fly at more than twenty-five times the speed of sound and have traveled to and from the moon on nine occasions. Here on Earth, however, where an atmosphere exists, we are forced to contend with its penalizing reality and continue to refine our newly found flying prowess.

Too often, advancements in the aforementioned disciplines of flight appear to be in a holding pattern, like an airliner above a busy airport. But when an advancement is discovered, developed, and ultimately put to flight-test, manned flight can—and often does—improve dramatically.

The first discipline of flight, aeronautics, is the actual design and construction of aircraft. It is the most basic and important element of manned flight.

The second discipline, aerodynamics, is the science that deals with the motion of gases and particularly with the atmospheric forces exerted on aircraft. Advancements in aerodynamic design have steadily improved the range, speed, maneuverability, and agility of aircraft by reducing the penalties imposed on aircraft by drag.

The third discipline, the airframe, is the complete interior and exterior structure of an aircraft. Aircraft airframes have evolved from wood-and-fabric to all-metal alloys such as aluminum, stainless steel, and titanium. And today, with the use of advanced composite materials, airframes for the current generation of aircraft—the B-2 stealth bomber and F-22 Advanced Tactical Fighter—are lighter and stronger.

The fourth major discipline, the powerplant, is the primary propulsion unit or units that propel aircraft, whether piston, turbojet, fanjet, or rocket power, or any combination thereof. Powerplants, too, have evolved to the point where they are as different as a Fokker Triplane and an F-16—from the first rotary engines that would barely keep the lightest fabric-covered plane aloft to light, extraordinarily powerful jet engines that allow modern

With test pilots like Jack Woolams (in the number-two XP-59A above), and "Tex" Johnston (in the number seven YP-59A below (now at the Planes of Fame Museum, Chino, California), the Bell Aircraft Corporation was able to develop America's first turbojet-powered airplane. Noteworthy are the rounded—versus squared—wing tips of the original and next type to find proper aerodynamic performance. *Bell Aerospace Textron*

As its Boeing B-52A mother ship heads for launch altitude, North American X-15A number three's LOX or liquid oxygen tanks are continuously topped off. Later, at some 45,000ft above northwestern Utah, it would be launched for its attack on speed and altitude records. During the X-15A/A-2 flight-test programs, a maximum speed of 4,520mph (Mach number 6.70) and a maximum altitude of 354,200ft were achieved over Edwards. *NASA*

fighters to take off and accelerate through Mach number 1 while flying straight upward.

For more than fifty years, since the 1940s, Edwards Air Force Base (AFB) has been an epicenter for revolutions in flight and a significant flight-test facility for investigating the critical disciplines of flight.

Edwards AFB is the home of the Air Force Flight Test Center (AFFTC), where the US Air Force and a number of other US Government agencies test, develop, and evaluate aircraft in the US inventory.

The AFFTC is an important component of the Air Force Materiel Command (AFMC), which has three primary responsibilities toward the US Air Force's combat readiness and national defense. The AFMC strives to advance aeronautical and space sciences and technologies, adapt these advances into development and improvements on operational systems, and acquire superior air power at the lowest possible cost.

Flight testing is carried out at Edwards to meet this triad of responsibilities. The AFFTC also conducts, supports, and participates in test and evaluation programs for other US Air Force units, the Department of Defense (DoD), the DoD's Advanced Research Projects Agency (ARPA), the National Aeronautics and Space Administration (NASA), and the US Army, Navy, and Marine Corps.

Located on the western edge of the Mojave Desert in the state of California, Edwards AFB is about 100mi northeast of Los Angeles, California.

Edwards' climate is dry with generally clear skies. Rain, which falls mostly from November through March, averages just 4in per year. Summer temperatures average around 100deg F., while nights are pleasantly cool. Winter daytime temperatures range from the mid-forties to the upper-sixties and rarely drop below freezing. Snowstorms are rare, but high-velocity windstorms and accompanying dust storms occur occasionally.

Due to Edwards' good year-round flying weather and location, it is an ideal place to test aircraft and an ideal landing site for space-shuttle flights. Rogers Dry Lake bed, a natural 44sq-mi *playa* (a flat area at the bottom of a desert basin, sometimes temporarily covered with water), serves as a perfect runway for many flight-test programs and a ready-made place for emergency landings. Countless lives and hundreds of military, commercial, and private aircraft have been saved by the use of this lake bed in emergency situations.

The 301,000sq-ac of Edwards AFB has approximately 785 military officers and nearly 3,600 military enlisted men and women, plus some 10,800 civilian employees. The base is also home for more than 6,400 dependent spouses and children of military personnel assigned to it, as of March 1995. Edwards was first used by the military—specifically, the US Army Air Corps—in September 1933 when a small advance party from March Field, Riverside, California, came to design and maintain a bombardment and gunnery range for the Air Corps. Four years later, most Air Corps squadrons were performing bombardment and gunnery maneuvers there.

At the outbreak of World War II, the south end of Muroc Dry Lake (now Rogers Dry Lake) was used for training P-38 Lighting fighter pilots and B-24 Liberator and B-25 Mitchell bomber crews. While the fighter pilots practiced air-to-air combat tactics, bomber-crew training included attacks on a full-scale 650ft model of a Japanese Navy heavy cruiser, dubbed the *Muroc Maru*. Bomber pilots and bombardiers used the wooden ship for identification, skip-bombing, and strafing practice. (The *Muroc Maru*. passed from landmark to legend in 1950 when it was "sunk" as a flight hazard to aircraft.)

Beginning in December 1941, at the north end of the dry lake, the US Army Air Forces (USAAF)—as the US Army Air Corps had been renamed on 20 June 1941—initiated the first of many first-flight events when it tested the Curtiss Model CW-29B, a flying mock-up of a proposed fighter that would later materialize as the Curtiss XP-55 Ascender.

Later, negotiations with the Muroc Bombing and Gunnery Range commanding officer, Maj. Glenn L. Arbogast, resulted in the assignment of the northern portion of the dry lake for exclusive use of Air Materiel Command (AMC) personnel who had been directed to proceed there and take charge of what was named the Materiel Center Flight Test Site.

In December 1942, the base was named the Materiel Command Flight Test Base. In 1944, it

was renamed the Muroc Flight Test Base. In October 1946, the Muroc Flight Test Base on the north end of Muroc Dry Lake and the bombing and gunnery crew training area on the south end of the dry lake merged. And, under AMC jurisdiction, it became Muroc Army Air Field (AAF).

Muroc AAF was redesignated Muroc AFB in February 1948. It became Edwards AFB in December 1949 in honor of Air Force Capt. Glen W. Edwards. A resident of Lincoln, California, Captain Edwards was killed on 5 June 1948 during a performance test of the experimental Northrop YB-49 Flying Wing. Official dedication of the newly named Edwards AFB took place on 27 January 1950.

Until 1950, US Air Force research and development had been the responsibility of the AMC. But in January 1950, the Air Research and Development Command (ARDC) was established as a new major command. During the next year-and-a-half, the ARDC absorbed practically all the research and development functions and installations previously assigned to the AMC.

Edwards AFB was one of the many installations transferred from the AMC to the newly formed ARDC on 2 April 1951. The AFFTC was activated at Edwards by the ARDC on 25 June 1951.

The AFFTC mission was to flight-test aircraft, operate special facilities, and provide facilities for contractors and other government agencies.

After a major reorganization in 1961, the ARDC became the Air Force Systems Command (AFSC). As part of the new command, the AFFTC was—and still is—responsible for research and development of the nation's aerospace weapons systems, from computer screen to operational readiness.

Through the years, the AFFTC has functioned as the focal point for testing and evaluating aircraft

and spacecraft concepts and designs. It has contributed directly to the improved combat capability of the US Air Force, as well as America's other armed forces. Many aerospace "firsts" occurred in the skies above Edwards AFB.

On 14 October 1947, US Air Force Capt. Charles E. "Chuck" Yeager became the first man to penetrate the once-feared sound barrier. He accomplished this feat while piloting an experimental rocket-powered airplane, the Bell X-1. This event and others led directly to the development of the supersonic US Air Force Century Series of jet-powered fighter aircraft, beginning with the North American F-100 Super Sabre.

Three North American X-15s, which are still the world's fastest and highest flying winged aircraft, were tested at Edwards AFB from mid-1959 to late 1968. Knowledge gained from the 199 X-15 flights hastened the day of America's manned orbital and moon flights.

The second X-15, now on permanent display at the Air Force Museum, Wright-Patterson AFB, Ohio, set an unofficial world speed record of 4,520mph (Mach number 6.70) on 3 October 1967. The third X-15, on 22 August 1963, reached an unofficial (because they were air-launched and did not takeoff under their own power) world record altitude of 354,200ft, making them the only airplanes ever to fly into space. These records still stand.

From 1964 to 1969 the world's first and only triple-sonic bomber airplane—the North American XB-70A Valkyrie, flew 128 times, reaching a top speed of 2,000mph (Mach number 3.08) and a maximum altitude of 74,000ft. The XB-70A was the largest and heaviest airplane to ever attain this kind of performance.

In mid 1965, the world's largest-ever manned interceptor—the Lockheed YF-12A, established several world's absolute speed and altitude records on the very same day at Edwards. These include a maximum speed of 2,070.102mph (Mach number 3.21) and a maximum altitude of 80,258ft.

The McDonnell Douglas F-15 Eagle, a high performance, extremely maneuverable fighter, made its first flight at Edwards on 27 July 1972. The F-15 is equipped with radar and defensive and offensive systems to detect, acquire, track, and attack any threat while operating in friendly or enemy-controlled airspace. Testing of the Eagle

The NASP (National Aero-Space Plane) if successful, will ultimately lead to the creation of future military trans-atmospheric vehicles or TAVs for orbital reconnaissance missions. This is an artist's rendering of what the turn-of-the-century NASP might look like. *Rockwell*

continues at the base, although the first operational F-15 was delivered to the US Air Force Tactical Air Command (TAC), now Air Combat Command (ACC), some twenty years ago.

Another high performance fighter still being tested at Edwards is the F-16 fighting Falcon. Its first flight occurred at the base in February 1974. The first production F-16 was accepted by the US Air Force in early 1979. Several North Atlantic Treaty Organization (NATO) countries also operate this highly maneuverable and agile fighter.

The B-1 bomber test program resumed at the AFFTC in early 1983 using two of the original four Rockwell B-1A aircraft, modified to the B-1B Lancer configuration. Changes to the offensive and defensive avionics systems, new weapons bay doors and bulkheads, as well as minor changes to external shaping to meet low-observable or stealth requirements were all part of B-1B modification program implemented by Rockwell.

The first production B-1B was rolled out of its Palmdale, California, assembly plant in late 1984. Its first flight, from Palmdale to Edwards, occurred on 19 October 1984. The first operational B-1B was delivered in June 1985.

Subsequent test programs such as the McDonnell Douglas C-17 Globemaster III, the Northrop B-2 Spirit, and the Rockwell-Deutsche Aerospace X-31 are current and ongoing.

Edwards AFB is where the nation's first jet- and rocket-powered flights took place. It is the place where men and aircraft first exceeded Mach numbers 1, 2, 3, 4, 5, and 6, and where they first flew above 100,000ft, 200,000ft, and 300,000ft.

Just as aviation's past is deeply rooted at Edwards, so is its future. Each time a pilot and his airplane challenge the unexplored and return, the knowledge gained is used as a stepping stone toward greater aerospace advances.

Over the years Edwards has become synonymous with aeronautical achievement. It is, as Dr. James O. Young, chief historian of the AFFTC History Office says, "the place where dreams come true."

The advanced technologies investigated at Edwards are proof that mankind's ongoing search for better ways to fly has not stalled. It might very well be that now the birds are watching *us*.

The XP-80 and its follow-on designs—the XP-80A and YP-80A—led to the production of combat-ready P-80A Shooting Star airplanes. The Lockheed P-80 holds the distinction of being America's first operational jet fighter. The one-of-a-kind XP-80 (shown after its restoration for permanent display) nicknamed *Lulu-Belle*, was powered by one de Havilland H.1B Goblin turbojet engine of British design. It only produced 2,460lb installed thrust, but it allowed the XP-80 to hit a top speed of almost 500mph; in fact, on one flight it achieved a top speed of 506mph, becoming the first jet-powered airplane in the United States to exceed 500mph. Piloted by Lockheed test pilot Milo Burcham, the XP-80 made its first flight on 8 January 1944. The single-place XP-80 has a wingspan of 37ft, a length of 32ft 10in, a height of 10ft 3in, and a gross weight of 8,620lb. The success of the XP-80 led to the production of 1,732 examples of the Shooting Star. *Lockheed*

Chapter 1

The Jet Age: the 1940s and 1950s

Following its rudimentary beginnings in the early 1930s, even before it was a bona fide airfield with paved runways, the so-called jet age at Edwards began in the early 1940s. By the end of the 1950s, the jet age had not only arrived, it was in full bloom. And it was the constant flight-test activities of newer and better experimental aircraft that would put Edwards AFB on the map of advanced-aerospace facilities.

In February 1942, USAAF Colonels Benjamin W. Chidlaw and Ralph P. Swofford of the AMC at Wright Field, Ohio, on an extended tour of the western United States, chose the north end of the dry lake as the ideal location to test the Bell XP-59A, a new and super-secret airplane, powered not by a conventional piston engine but by a new and unconventional gas turbine, or turbojet engine.

In September 1942, America's first jet airplane arrived at the site. Shipped cross-country by rail in crates from Bell's Buffalo, New York, facility, it was uncrated and readied for its first flight. The XP-59A, later named Airacomet, made its first flight on 2 October 1942. As flight-testing of the XP-59A progressed, it became apparent that the location was perfect for such activities.

With the advent of such notable jet aircraft as the F-80 Shooting Star, first tested as the Lockheed XP-80; the F-84 Thunderjet, first evaluated as the Republic XP-84; the F-86 Sabre Jet, first probed as the North American XP-86; and the B-45 Tornado, first judged as the North American XB-45, it is simple to realize the value of just such a flight-test facility as it was in the 1940s.

And in the 1950s with the creation of other notable jet aircraft as the A-4 Skyhawk, first tested as the Douglas XA4D-1; the F-100 Super Sabre, first evaluated as the North American YF-100; the F-104 Starfighter, first judged as the Lockheed XF-104; the F-8 Crusader, first investigated as the Chance Vought XF8U-1; and the F-5 Freedom Fighter, first proved by the Northrop Model N-156F, it becomes even easier to see the advantages of a first-class aviation evaluation center.

By the end of the 1950s, in little less than two full decades, the US Air Force, NASA (formerly National Advisory Committee for Aeronautics or NACA), US Navy, and other government agencies had enjoyed significant gains in piston-, turbojet-, turbopropjet-, and rocket-powered air vehicle performances.

From the maiden flight of America's premier jet-powered airplane—the Bell XP-59A Airacomet— to the initial flights of what would become the fastest and highest flying rocket-powered airplane—the North American X-15—manned air vehicles had already exceeded 2,000mph (Mach number 3) and the altitude of 125,000ft. As great as these marks were, in just another ten years, they were shattered. That is: speeds of 2,700mph (Mach number 4), 3,400mph (Mach number 5), and 4,200mph (Mach number 6) were attained. Moreover, altitudes of 150,000ft, 200,000ft, and 300,000ft were surpassed—culminating with maximums of 4,520mph (Mach number 6.70), and 354,200ft.

More important for national security, US combat aircraft flown on a daily basis were now capable of supersonic and doublesonic speeds in level-attitude flight and could reach altitudes near 70,000ft. These advances in performance could not have been realized without the "country and duty" philosophies of the many dedicated flight-test personnel at Edwards AFB. Patriots one and all, they just saluted, or said, "Yes sir," and did their jobs. As they do today.

For their respective contributions some of these flight-test pilots like Chuck Yeager, Frank Everest, and Tony LeVier have become famous. Others like George Welch, Mel Apt, Milo Burcham, and Glen Edwards famed on their own merits—contributed their lives. This is what legendary men, living or not, are all about. The living are timeless; the non-living are immortal. Each and every one of us, for what they have done for this nation, owe these brave men our personal gratitude.

It was the above-mentioned men, and the others, that made it so exciting at Edwards in the 1940s and 1950s.

The Bell P-59 Airacomet was America's first turbojet-powered airplane. Developed under Secret Project MX-397 during World War II, the airplane's basic mission was to be the pursuit, interception, and destruction of enemy aircraft. Although it was developed and produced in time for such action, it proved to be too slow (some contemporary piston-powered fighters were faster) for operational status. Thus, instead of going into combat, it remained in the United States as a jet trainer for the duration of the war. Designed to fight at 500mph-plus speeds, the P-59B (the last production model) was powered by two 1,425lb-thrust General Electric J31-GE-5 engines, which only gave the type a best all-out speed of 400mph. The single-place XP-59A has a wingspan of 49ft, a length of 38ft 10in (with cannon), a height of 12ft 4in, and a gross weight of 10,500lb. Combat P-59s were to be armed with one 37mm cannon and three .50cal machine guns—all nose-mounted; they could have carried two under-wing 100lb bombs (one under either wing). Shown is the second XP-59A during one of its many test flights over Muroc. *Bell Aerospace Textron*

The XP-80 and its follow-on designs—the XP-80A and YP-80A—led to the production of combat-ready P-80A Shooting Star airplanes. The Lockheed P-80 holds the distinction of being America's first operational jet fighter. The one-of-a-kind XP-80 (shown after its restoration for permanent display) nicknamed *Lulu-Belle*, was powered by one de Havilland H.1B Goblin turbojet engine of British design. It only produced 2,460lb installed thrust, but it allowed the XP-80 to hit a top speed of almost 500mph; in fact, on one flight it achieved a top speed of 506mph, becoming the first jet-powered airplane in the United States to exceed 500mph. Piloted by Lockheed test pilot Milo Burcham, the XP-80 made its first flight on 8 January 1944. The single-place XP-80 has a wingspan of 37ft, a length of 32ft 10in, a height of 10ft 3in, and a gross weight of 8,620lb. The success of the XP-80 led to the production of 1,732 examples of the Shooting Star. *Lockheed*

The Douglas XB-43 was America's first turbojet-powered bomber, and it was powered by the first jet engine designed and built in the United States—the General Electric Model TG-180 or J35. The XB-43 was developed under Project MX-475, and two XB-43s were built (the number-two airplane is shown). After being towed to Muroc AAF on 28 January 1946, the first XB-43, flown by Douglas test pilots Bob Brush and Russ Thaw, made its first flight on 17 May 1946. Classified as a light bomber plane—it could only carry a 4,000lb bomb load—the XB-43 has a wingspan of 71ft 2in, a length of 51ft 2in, a height of 24ft 3in, and a gross weight of 39,530lb; its top speed at sea level was 515mph. The number-one XB-43 crash-landed on 1 February 1951; grounded, its parts were used to keep number two flying as an engine test-bed. On 30 October 1953, after its retirement, the number-two XB-43 was flown from Edwards to Bolling AFB, near Washington, D.C., where it was presented to the National Air and Space Museum. *AFFTC/HO*

First flown on 25 June 1946—from Hawthorne, California, to Muroc AAF—the Northrop XB-35 Flying Wing bomber was developed under Secret Project MX-140. The all-wing B-35 was powered by four piston-type 3,000hp Pratt & Whitney R-4360-17 or -21 Wasp Major engines with dual four-bladed, contra-rotating propellers. The XB-35 has a wingspan of 172ft (identical to today's B-2), a length of 53ft 1in, a height of 20ft 1in, and a gross weight of 180,000lb. Operational B-35s were to carry a 10,000lb bomb load up to 5,000mi and return. A second type, the only completed YB-35 (shown), made its first flight on 15 May 1948. It was the only one equipped with machine gun turrets, sans guns. The XB-35 was in direct competition with Convair's XB-36. Because its range, payload, and stability as a bombardment platform were inferior to the XB-36's, Northrop's B-35 program was terminated in 1949. With the exception of the three B-35 airframes that were converted into two eight-jet YB-49s and one six-jet YRB-49A, all B-35 airframes were scrapped. *AFFTC/HO*

On 12 September 1946, with Wallace A. Lien at the controls, the first of three North American XFJ-1 Furys made its first flight at Muroc. Developed as a US Navy carrier fighter, the Fury was powered by one non-afterburning 4,000lb-thrust-class General Electric J35 turbojet engine. Its top speed was 545mph at 12,000ft. Development of the three prototypes led to a production batch of only thirty FJ-1s, and they served with VF-5A on the USS *Boxer* until October 1949; seventy on order were canceled. The production FJ-1 with wing-tip fuel tanks has a wingspan of 39ft 2in, a length of 33ft 5in, a height of 14ft 10in, and a gross weight of 15,100lb. The standard armament was six nose-mounted .50cal machine guns, but none of them ever fired a shot in combat. The FJ-1 shown is an early production Fury. The "B" on the nose denotes that it is from the carrier *Boxer*. Having a short-lived career, mainly because of their straight wings and limited engine thrust, the XFJ-1 and FJ-1 furies led to the development of the swept-winged and much-improved FJ-2, FJ-3, and FJ-4 series of Furys. *Rockwell*

Powered by four non-afterburning 4,00lb-thrust-class Allison J35-A-7 turbojet engines, the first of two North American XB-45 Tornado prototype bombers (shown) made its first flight at Muroc on 17 March 1947. First flown by North American test pilot George Krebs, the XB-45 has a wingspan of 89ft 6in, a length of 74ft, a height of 25ft 2in, and a gross weight of 66,800lb. The Tornado could carry up to 8,000lb of bombs (sixteen 500lb). As nuclear weapons got smaller and lighter, however, the B-45 became fully capable of carrying a single atomic bomb. Moreover, production B-45s were powered by up-rated 5,000lb-thrust-class General Electric J47 turbojet engines. The XB-45 has a top speed of 515mph at 14,000ft with the Allison J35s. Production B-45s, with the General Electric J47s, had a top speed near 600mph at best altitude. *Rockwell*

The first of three Douglas D-558-1 Skystreak aircraft (shown) made its first flight at Muroc on 15 April 1947. First flown by Douglas test pilot Gene May, it was powered by one non-afterburning 5,000lb-thrust Allison J35-A-11 turbojet engine. As a high-speed research airplane for the Navy, the number-one Skystreak established two world speed records at Muroc, on 20 and 25 August 1947. The first, 640.663mph, was set by Cdr. Turner Caldwell; the second, 650.796mph, was established by Marine Corps Maj. Marion Carl. The single-seat Skystreak has a wingspan of 25ft, a length of 35ft 8-1/2in, a height of 12ft 2in, and a gross weight of 10,100lb. Its top speed at sea level was 651mph, as demonstrated with the speed record at low-altitude over a 3km (1.6mi) course at Muroc in 1947. Nicknamed the "Flying Stovepipe" for obvious reason the D-558-1 was jointly tested by the Navy, the Marine Corps, and NACA before retirement. Skystreak number two crashed on 3 May 1948, killing NACA pilot Howard C. Lilly. The two remaining Skystreaks are on permanent display at aviation museums—the first at the Naval Aviation Museum at Pensacola, Florida, and the third at Marine Corps Air Station Quantico, Virginia. *McDonnell Douglas*

First flown on 1 October 1947 at Muroc, the first of three North American XP-86 Sabre aircraft poses above the base. Optimized from the start to be a daytime air-superiority fighter, the swept-wing Sabre was just that during the Korean War, flown by thirty-nine of the forty American aces (five or more kills) of that war. Powered by one non-afterburning 4,000lb-thrust General Electric or Allison J35 turbojet engine, the XP-86 has a top speed of 618mph at 14,000ft. Production F-86s, powered by single, afterburning 5,900lb-thrust General Electric J47 turbojets, were able to attain 690mph speeds at sea level. The single-seat XP-86 (XF-86 after 10 June 1948) has a wingspan of 37ft 1in, a length of 37ft 6in, a height of 14ft 9in, and a gross weight of 13,800lb. First flown by North American chief test pilot George Welch, the XP/XF-86 led to the ultimate production of more than 6,200 Sabre Jets in seven different versions—the F-86A, F-86D, F-86E, F-86F, F-86H, F-86K, and F-86L. The A, E, F, and H models were fighters, and the D, K, and L versions were interceptors. Armed with six .50cal machine guns, the F-86 was indeed a gunfighter during the Korean War. With an announced kill ratio of more than ten-to-one, the Sabre's dominance in combat gave rise to the phrase: "You're '86'd!" Maybe you've heard it. *Rockwell*

Developed under Project MX-51, the first of two Northrop YB-49 Flying Wing bomber prototypes made its first flight—Hawthorne to Muroc AFB—on 21 October 1947. Powered by eight 3,800lb-thrust Allison J35-A-15 turbojet engines, the YB-49's top speed was 493mph at 20,800ft. The YB-49, with a combat radius of 1,615mi with 10,00lb of bombs, had a wingspan of 172ft (identical to the B-2 of today), a length of 53ft 1in, a height of 15ft 2in, and a gross weight of 193,940lb. Unfortunately, both YB-49s were lost. The number-two YB-49 was destroyed in June 1948, killing its five-man crew,

including Capt. Glen W. Edwards, for whom Edwards AFB was renamed. The number-one YB-49 was demolished in March 1950 during a high-speed taxi test; its crew survived. Another version of the YB-49, the one-of-a-kind, six-jet YRB-49A flew until its retirement in 1951. With the demise of the B-35, B-49, and RB-49 programs, John K. "Jack" Northrop's dream of flying-wing bombers sailing through the skies of the world was over. That is until the design was reborn in the guise of the Northrop B-2A Spirit, which is now operational. *Northrop*

The first of three Douglas D-558-2 Skyrocket aircraft made its first flight at Muroc on 4 February 1948. It was flown by Douglas test pilot John F. "Johnnie" Martin. With its swept-back wings and tails, and its higher-thrust turbojet engine, it was a direct follow-on to the Douglas D-558-1 Skystreak. Designed from the start to take off under its own power, its true performance capabilities were not realized until it was modified for aerial launches with the addition of rocket propulsion. It was then when the Skyrocket lived up to its name, becoming the first manned airplane to fly at doublesonic speed (1,325mph [Mach number 2.005] on 20 November 1953), and above 80,000ft—when on 21 August 1953, it was flown to 83,235ft. Initially powered by one non-afterburning

3,000lb-thrust-class Westinghouse J34-WE-40 turbojet engine, the Skyrocket was modified to boost its performance with one four-chamber 6,000lb-thrust Reaction Motors XLR8-RM-5/-6 rocket motor. On turbojet power alone, the D-558-2's top speed was 545mph at 20,000ft. Being the same size, all three Skyrockets had a wingspan of 25ft, a length of 42ft, and a height of 12ft 8in. Launch weight with composite propulsion was 15,260lb. Before rocket power became available to the D-558-2, since its Westinghouse J34 only produced 3,000lb-thrust, it was forced to lift off from the lake bed with the aid of four (two have not fired yet) rocket-assisted take-off (RATO) units to conserve jet fuel. *McDonnell Douglas*

Lockheed built two XF-90 aircraft to compete against two McDonnell XF-88 aircraft for the US Air Force's Penetration Fighter program. The first XF-90 (shown) made its official first flight on 4 June 1949 at Edwards AFB with Lockheed test pilot Anthony W. "Tony" LeVier at the controls. The single-place XF-90 had a wingspan of 40ft, a length of 56ft 2in, a height of 15ft 9in, and a gross weight of 31,060lb. Ultimately powered by two afterburning 4,200lb-thrust Westinghouse J34-WE-15 turbojet engines (it was initially powered by two non-afterburning J34-WE-11 engines), the XF-90 had a top speed of 668mph (Mach number 0.99) in level flight; 739mph (Mach number 1.12) in a dive. The Penetration Fighter contest was held at Edwards from 29 June to 7 July 1950. It involved a fly-off between the XF-90, the XF-88, and a late entry, the North American YF-93. McDonnell's XF-88 was the winner, as announced by the Air Force on 11 September 1950. Ultimately, with many alterations, the XF-88 was developed into the F-101 Voodoo. Neither the XF-90 nor YF-93 were developed further. *Lockheed*

With Lockheed test pilot Tony LeVier under glass, the first of two YF-94C (formerly YF-97A) service-test planes (shown) made its first flight at Edwards on 19 January 1950. Developed as an all-rocket-armed fighter-interceptor from the all-machine gun-armed F-94B fighter, this version of the Lockheed Starfire was powered by an afterburning 9,000lb-thrust-class Pratt & Whitney J48-P-5 turbojet engine and was capable of near-650mph speed in level flight. The two-place F-94C Starfire had a wingspan of 42ft 5in, a length of 44ft 6in, a height of 15ft, and a gross weight of 19,000lb. Production F-94Cs were armed with forty-eight 2.75in-diameter Mighty Mouse unguided rockets—twenty-four in the nose and twelve in a pod on each wing. The service-test YF-94Cs did not have the wing-mounted rocket pods. *Lockheed*

Next page
Armament-test is another function of Edwards AFB. Here, in late 1950, an early production North American F-86D Sabre was being prepared for a test of its only armament—twenty-four unguided 2.75in-diameter Mighty Mouse folding-fin rockets. This particular D-version of the famous Sabre line was the dedicated armament test-bed for the type (note camera housings and lens windows). Powered by one afterburning General Electric J47 turbojet engine, the F-86D was capable of more than 690mph speed. With its radar and fire control system, it was capable of limited all-weather operation as an interceptor. The first D, one of two YF-86D aircraft, was first flown at Edwards on 22 December 1949 by North American test pilot George Welch. Originally known as the YF-95A, the YF-86D had a wingspan of 37ft 1in, a length of 40ft 3in, a height of 15ft, and a gross weight of 13,400lb. *Rockwell*

Developed under Secret Project MX-743, the Bell X-2 was designed and built to investigate the high-speed, high-altitude flying characteristics of swept-back flying surfaces. Although the X-2 eventually broke world speed and altitude records (2,094mph or Mach number 3.196, and 125,907ft), its flight-test career at Edwards only involved twenty flights from 27 June 1951 to 27 September 1956. Two X-2s were built, each one powered by one throttleable, two-chamber Curtiss-Wright XLR25-CW-1 or -3 rocket motor that was fueled with a combination of water, alcohol, and liquid oxygen. The two-chamber motor produced a variable thrust rating of 2,500–15,000lb. The single-place X-2 had a wingspan of 32ft 3in, a length of 45ft 5in, a height of 12ft, and a gross weight of 24,910lb. Sadly, three men lost their lives during the X-2 flight-test program. From a wing-mounted camera, X-2 number one is shown returning to base after its first glide flight on 5 August 1954. *USAF*

Developed under Secret Project MX-656 as a turbojet-powered research airplane, designed to investigate aerodynamic heating (thermodynamics) of an airframe flying at least 30min at doublesonic speeds, the one-of-a-kind Douglas X-3 made a successful first flight at Edwards on 20 October 1952, with Douglas test pilot Bill Bridgeman at the controls. The single-seat Stiletto (now at the US Air Force Museum, Dayton, Ohio) has a wingspan of 22ft 8-1.4in, a length of 66ft 9in, a height of 12ft 7in, and a gross weight of 22,400lb. Powered by two afterburning 4,850lb-thrust Westinghouse J34-WE-17 turbojet engines instead of the planned-for two afterburning 7,000lb-thrust Westinghouse J46-WE-1 turbojets, the X-3 was woefully under-powered. The result being that it could not even fly at supersonic speed unless it was dived from high altitude. Without adequate propulsion, the airplane was retired from flight status after fifty-one total flights. Though it never performed the duties it was built to do, its unique configuration (short wings and a long knife-like fuselage) later contributed to the success of other aircraft, one being the stubby-winged Lockheed F-104. *McDonnell Douglas*

The number-one XB-51 (shown) arrived at Edwards on 28 February 1953. Powered by three afterburning 5,200lb-thrust General Electric J47-GE-13 turbojet engines (one on each side of the fuselage near the nose section and one in the tail). the XB-51 had a top speed of 645mph at sea level. The two-place XB-51 had a wingspan of 53ft 1in, a length of 85ft 1in, a height of 17ft 4in, and a gross weight (with a 4,000lb bomb load) of 55,920lb. The number-one XB-51, which starred as the "XF-120 Gilbert Fighter" in the Warner Brothers movie *Toward the Unknown*, crashed to destruction on 25 March 1956 near El Paso, Texas, during the movie's filming. The number-two XB-51 crashed to destruction on 9 May 1952 at Edwards killing its only crewman, Maj. Neil H. Lathrop of the US Air Force, then chief of the flight-test branch at Edwards. With the advent of the 600mph Boeing B-47 Stratojet and its heavier bomb load, there was no need for production B-51s, so the project was terminated. Nevertheless, with its Martin-developed rotary-action bomb rack and other innovations, the XA-45-/XB-51 played an important role in the development of US jet bomber aircraft, including the B-1 and B-2, which have rotary-action bomb racks. *AFFTC/HO*

First flown at Edwards on 25 May 1953 by North American chief test pilot George Welch, the first of two YF-100 Super Sabre prototypes (shown) exceeded the speed of sound in level flight (Mach number 1.10 or 745mph at 35,000ft). Supersonic flight speeds were not new in 1953, but in level flight, by a combat-type airplane, they sure were. And to prove it wasn't a fluke, he did it again on a second test hop that very same day. Powered by one afterburning 13,200lb-thrust Pratt & Whitney YJ57-P-7 turbojet engine, the YF-100 ultimately attained a speed of 890mph (Mach number 1.3). The single-seat YF-100 had a wingspan of 36ft 7in, a length of 47ft 1-1/4in, a height of 16ft 3in, and a gross weight of 24,780lb. The F-100 has the distinction of being the first of the so-called Century Series of jet-powered Air Force fighters. One of these, the North American F-107 Ultra Sabre, was in fact derived from the F-100 Super Sabre. Due to the success of the two YF-100s, in all North American went on to produce more than 2,300 Super Sabres in four versions—the F-100A, F-100C, F-100D, and F-100F. *Rockwell*

Developed under Weapon System 303A, the Lockheed F-104 Starfighter's primary mission was that of a high-speed, high-altitude (with a rapid climb rate) air-superiority day fighter. Though its mission was later changed to that of an air-defense fighter-interceptor, it retained its dog-fight capability. The first of two XF-104s was first powered by an interim non-afterburning Wright J65 turbojet engine. Later, with an afterburning version of the interim J65 engine, the second XF-104 (shown) hit a top speed of 1,150mph (Mach number 1.79). First flown at Edwards on 5 March 1954 (the official first flight date) by famed Lockheed test pilot Tony LeVier, the XF-104 became the first jet-powered airplane in the world to exceed 1,000mph (Mach number 1.52) in level flight. Dubbed the "missile with a man in it," due to its rocket-like shape, the F-104 holds the distinction of being the worlds first doublesonic fighter. The single-place XF-104 had a wingspan of 22ft 9in (without wing-tip fuel tanks), a length of 49ft 1in, a height of 13ft 4in, and a gross weight of 16,700lb. Both XF-104s crashed to destruction during their careers. Their success, however, led to the production of more than 2,575 F-104s. *Lockheed*

On 23 August 1954, with Lockheed test pilots Stanley Betz (pilot) and Roy Wimmer (copilot) at the controls, the second of two service-test Lockheed YC-130 Hercules aircraft made its first flight—Burbank, California, to Edwards AFB. Number two (shown) flew before number one because the first example was used for static-test before it was later flown. Powered by four 3,250eshp (estimated shaft horsepower) Allison T56-A-1 turbopropjet engines spinning three-bladed propellers, the YC-130's top speed was 380mph at 20,500ft. It has a wingspan of 132ft 6in, a length of 97ft 8in, a height of 38ft 5in, and a gross weight of 125,000lb. Classified as a medium-lift tactical transport, the C-130 Hercules is still in production, now being produced as the C-130J, with new engines spinning all-composite six-bladed propellers. Lockheed has built more than 2,000 C-130s. *Lockheed*

After it was shipped to Edwards from Chance Vought Aircraft's Dallas, Texas, plant in March 1955, the first of two XF8U-1 Crusader prototypes was prepared for flight. On 25 March, with Chance Vought test pilot John W. Konrad at the controls, the first Crusader lifted-off on its maiden flight. Powered by one afterburning 14,800lb-thrust Pratt & Whitney J57-P-11 turbojet engine, the number-one XF8U-1 hit a top speed of 700mph (Mach number 1.05) at 35,000ft in level-attitude flight. The single-place XF8U-1 Crusader (now at the Museum of Flight in Seattle, Washington) has a wingspan of 35ft 8in, a length of 54ft 3in, a height of 13ft 4in, and a gross weight of 25,500lb. Ordered into full-scale production, the Crusader was the first operational aircraft-carrier fighter in the world to exceed 1,000mph (Mach number 1.52), and it established several world speed records. Moreover, during air-to-air combat in the Vietnam War—because it had retained guns when most other US fighters were armed only with missiles, the Crusader had a fantastic kill ratio against the MiG-17s and MiG-21s flown by the North Vietnamese. Shown is *One-X* (the nickname of XF8U-1 number one) during its first flight with Konrad under glass. *AFFTC/HO*

Developed under Weapon System 306A, the Republic F-105 Thunderchief's main mission was that of an all-weather, supersonic fighter-bomber for the US Air Force's Tactical Air Command (now Air Combat Command). Moreover, it had to be capable of performing the air-superiority role, and it had to be able to carry and deliver a "special," or nuclear weapon. Powered by an interim, afterburning 15,000lb-thrust Pratt & Whitney J57-P-25 turbojet engine on that first flight, it hit 710mph (Mach number 1.05) at 30,000ft in level-attitude flight. Later, with NASA's Area Rule application to eliminate unwanted drag in the transonic speed regime (600–800mph) and with the more-powerful, afterburning 25,500lb-thrust Pratt & Whitney J75-P-3 turbojet engine, the subsequent YF-105Bs (four were built; number three is shown), easily romped to 1,541mph (Mach number 2.3). In the end, as a doublesonic tactical fighter-bomber and air-superiority fighter, the F-105 was a success. Its ability finally led to the production of more than 800 Thunderchiefs in three basic models: the F-105B, F-105D and F-105F. It was the last fighter produced by the Republic Aviation Corporation. *AFFTC/HO*

The "Rocking Fifties" at Edwards played host to the US Air Force's Century Series of six different turbojet-powered fighter aircraft as shown here from above. Clockwise from the left these included the Convair F-106 Delta Dart, North American F-100 Super Sabre, McDonnell F-101 Voodoo, Convair F-102 Delta Dagger, Lockheed F-104 Starfighter, and the Republic F-105 Thunderchief. Three of them (F-100, F-101, and F-102) were powered by the Pratt & Whitney J57 engine; two of them (F-105 and F-106) were powered by the Pratt & Whitney J75 engine; and one (F-104) was powered by the General Electric J79 engine—all hallmarks. Three (F-100, F-101, and F-102) were capable of level-flight supersonic speeds, and three (F-104, F-105, and F-106) were capable of level-flight doublesonic speeds. After their respective flight-test programs at Edwards, each type became operational and had fine careers before they were retired. *AFFTC/HO*

A seventh Century Series fighter—the North American F-107 Ultra Sabre, appeared at Edwards in late 1956. Powered by one afterburning 24,500lb-thrust Pratt & Whitney J75-P-9 turbojet engine, the first of three F-107 aircraft (shown) made its first flight on 10 September 1956 with North American test pilot J. Robert "Bob" Baker at the controls. Developed as a dual-role airplane—that is, it pulled double duty as an air-superiority fighter and a fighter bomber—it competed with Republic's F-105 Thunderchief. Following a very hard-fought competition, the Thunderchief prevailed, and the F-107 became a foot note in aviation history. Still, with its unique dorsal inlet system and top speed of 1,541mph (Mach number 2.3), it was not immediately put out to pasture. Because of the Ultra Sabre's speed, NASA used two of them for several years at Edwards to bolster its aeronautical knowledge. Despite its capabilities, the F-107 was not a significant leap ahead in the so-called state of the art. However, both the Air Force and the NASA got their money's worth out of the three F-107 aircraft as they did provide valuable flight-test information during the late 1950s. *Rockwell*

The main mission of the McDonnell F-101B Voodoo, developed under Weapon System 217, was that of all-missile-armed all-weather air-defense interceptor. The first F-101B (shown), after a successful first flight at McDonnell's St. Louis, Missouri, facility on 27 March 1957, was ferried to Edwards for ongoing flight-test and armament-evaluation activities. The tandem-seat F-101B had a wingspan of 39ft 8in, a length of 71ft 1in, a height of 18ft, and a gross weight of 45,460lb. Powered by two afterburning 17,000lb-thrust-class Pratt & Whitney J57-P-55 turbojet engines, the B-Voodoo had a top speed of 1,100mph (Mach number 1.69) at 35,000ft. The all-missile-armed F-101B was very similar to the all-cannon-armed F-101A. It could carry two Douglas AIR-2 Genie nuclear air-to-air unguided rockets or three Hughes AIM-4 Falcon air-to-air guided missiles. The first F-101A, with McDonnell test pilot Bob Little at the controls, made its first flight at Edwards on 29 September 1954. Little also made the first flight of the first F-101B. *McDonnell Douglas.*

With Chance Vought test pilot John Konrad at the controls, the first of two XF8U-3 Crusader III (Super Crusader) prototype all-missile-armed interceptors made a successful first flight at Edwards on 2 June 1958. In competition with the McDonnell XF4H-1 Phantom II, the Super Crusader was powered by one afterburning 25,000lb-thrust-class Pratt & Whitney J75-P-6 turbojet engine; it was capable of 1,625mph (Mach number 2.4) in level-attitude flight. The single-seat XF8U-3 had a wingspan of 39 ft 11in, a length of 58ft 11in, a height of 16ft 5in, and a gross weight of 37,850lb. At the time, the US Navy preferred tandem-seat, twin-engine fighter aircraft. Since the XF8U-1 was a single-place, single-engine design with less armament (one less missile), the Phantom II was ordered into production. *Vought Aircraft*

Next page
After its 15 October 1958 roll-out ceremony at North American's Los Angeles facility, the first of three X-15 aircraft (shown) was trucked to Edwards; it arrived two days later. On 10 March 1959, with North American X-15 project pilot A. Scott Crossfield strapped-in, it completed its first captive-carry flight under the right wing of its B-52 carrier aircraft. On 8 June 1959, again with Crossfield at the controls, it made its first glide flight after being released from its mother plane. Just gliding, it hit a speed of 522mph (Mach number 0.79) from its release altitude of 37,550ft. Developed under US Air Force Project MX-1226, the X-15 has a wingspan of 22ft 3in, and overall length of 50ft, a height of 11ft 6in, and a gross weight of 31, 275lb. Since the planned-for 57,850lb-thrust (at 100,000ft) Reaction Motors XLR99 rocket motor was not yet available to the X-15 program, the first X-15 was temporarily powered by two 8,000lb-thrust Reaction Motors XLR11 rocket motors. It hit a maximum speed of 1,455mph (Mach number 2.11) and a peak altitude of 52,341ft during that first powered flight—but more, much more, was to be gained by the X-15s in the 1960s. *Rockwell*

From 25 January 1946 to 6 November 1958 at Edwards, the USAAF and NACA extensively evaluated three different types of Bell X-1 rocket-powered air vehicles. These included the X-1 (first generation), the X-1A/B/D (second generation), and the X-1E. The Bell X-1E, shown on its pylon outside the DFRF headquarters building at Edwards in late 1992, was tested from 12 December 1955 to 6 November 1958. During that time period, it was flown twenty-six times, and during those flights, it attained a best speed of 1,455mph (Mach number 2.24) and a best altitude of 75,000ft-plus. Two NACA pilots—Joe Walker (twenty-one flights) and John McKay (five flights)—were the only pilots to fly the one-of-a-kind X-1E. Powered by one four-chamber 6,000lb-thrust-class Reaction Motors LR8-RM-5 rocket motor (an advanced version of the LR11-RM-5 used to power earlier versions of the X-1), the X-1E has a wingspan of 22ft 10in, a length of 31ft, a height of 10ft 10in, and a gross weight of 14,750lb. For added stability at high speeds, the X-1E had ventral fins (now removed). *Author*

The Northrop Freedom Fighter was developed as a low-cost, lightweight fighter for friendly nations. Using its own funds, Northrop proceeded to build one Model N-156F demonstrator airplane (shown). On 30 June 1959, with Northrop test pilot Lewis A. "Lew" Nelson at the stick and rudder pedals, it made a successful first flight at Edwards AFB. Powered by two afterburning 4,000lb-thrust-class General Electric J85-GE-13 turbojet engines, the small fighter demonstrated supersonic speeds in level-attitude flight. Suddenly, Northrop had produced a less expensive and less complicated supersonic fighter that turned heads, even the heads of the US Air Force, who had at first rejected Northrop's offer outright. The YF-5A Freedom Fighter has a wingspan of 25ft 10in, a length of 47ft 2in, a height of 13ft 2in, and a gross weight of 13,450lb. The first YF-5A, in its original Model N-156F colors, now hangs from the ceiling of the Museum of Flight in Seattle. *Northrop*

Supersonic Flight From One Pilot's Point of View

by William B. "Bill" Bridgeman

Actually the US Navy's Douglas-built D-558-2 Skyrocket is now an obsolete aircraft. She was designed as a sort of follow-on to the US Navy's D-558 Skystreak, which was the first research type of airplane built by the Douglas Aircraft Company. Shortly after the straight-winged Skystreak research project began, the advantages of swept-back wings for aircraft operating in the transonic speed regime [600–800mph] began to be realized. It was therefore considered prudent to modify the original contract to include the investigation of swept-back flying surfaces [wings, vertical stabilizer, and horizontal stabilizer] in addition to the straight-winged configuration of the record-setting Skystreak. Since the full realization of the advantages of the swept-back flying surfaces at high speeds could not be obtained using even the most powerful turbojet engine available, it was found necessary to employ a supplementary rocket motor. Purposely, the airfoil sections of the Skyrocket are of the conventional subsonic type—that is, with rounded leading- and trailing-edges and contours, and not of the sharply angled chisel-point-type of airfoil sections employed for supersonic speeds. The purpose of the Skyrocket is to explore the upper limits of this type of airfoil which permits the retention of relatively normal low-speed flying characteristics [subsonic speeds between the aircraft's normal stall speed and about 600mph].

A great deal of turbojet-only flight-test activities were completed before the combined turbojet/rocket motor air-launched flight-test program was conceived. After Douglas chief test pilot John F. "Johnnie" Martin had completed numerous slow-speed stability and control tests on the Skyrocket program, a Reaction Motors, Incorporated rocket motor [a 6,000lb-thrust XLR8-RM-5] was installed and Douglas test pilot Eugene F. "Gene" May did the first flight-test duties to prove out this experimental motor. After the Skyrocket airframe and composite powerplant combination was

Bill Bridgeman.

approved for air-launched flight-test activities, an aerial-launch airplane, a Boeing B-29 Superfortress, was put to work.

The advantage of the additional thrust made available by the rocket motor was immediately realized and a new peak Mach number above 1.0 was the result. However, as testing progressed, it became more and more obvious that the airplane's turbojet [a 3,000lb-thrust Westinghouse J34-WE-40] and rocket motor was not a compatible combination. Simply because the thrust from the non-air-breathing rocket motor made it possible for the Skyrocket to take the air-breathing turbojet engine to heights where there wasn't enough oxygen to keep it resuscitated, and to speeds for which it was not designed to operate at. [To produce thrust efficiently, all turbojet engines require that intake air entering their compressor section is traveling at subsonic speed.] This, of course, would complicate and reduce flight-test data immensely and dictated that a very careful post-flight analysis was required of the test pilot, aerodynamicist, and propulsion engineers.

One instance I have in mind was a flight in which the airplane was flown to a rather high altitude using turbojet thrust by itself. After leveling off, the rocket motor chambers [four] were fired in sequence. And subsequently, the airplane reached the edge of its buffet boundary. This meant there was a natural and moderate shaking of the airframe. But when the plane continued to vibrate after the pilot's retreat from the buffet zone had been made, some concern set in. Inspection of the turbojet engine instruments on the dash revealed the tailpipe temperature was some 75deg F. over that permitted. Manipulation of the engine throttle brought things back under control. A following investigation found a compressor stall had been induced by the aircraft's altitude and Mach number which had caused the Skyrocket to vibrate and surpass the expected and natural buffeting to be found within the buffet boundary of the air vehicle.

Among the more memorable flights I made with the plane were in the maximum-climb-study portion of the program prior to the air-launched flights. On one such flight, immediately after takeoff and as soon as the airplane was clean [landing gear and flaps retracted], I simultaneously fired-off all four chambers of the rocket motor. The result of this action was that I had to bring the plane to an extremely sharp climbing angle of about 70deg to help hold its speed down low enough to stay out of the high-drag rise. That flight, and others like it, were wild rides! It seemed no matter how high a climbing angle was reached—even near 90deg vertical—the airspeed continued to build up. Finally, when I was almost flat on my back looking straight up in the sky, the speed would stabilize. Literally to me, to borrow an old phrase, it was somewhat like having a tiger by the tail. I felt as if all of the power on earth was driving me right up through a hole in the sky. It was really a lot of fun for me since I like to travel in such a manner.

But once more the turbojet complicated the picture. For at a time when a pilot's attention is needed elsewhere in the cockpit, constant attention had to be paid to the turbojet engine to keep it from over-speeding. Even though it was governed to no more than 500rpm below full military power, the speed of the plane produced by the rocket motor's power forced the turbojet to operate at its upper rpm limits; thus, tailpipe overheating. In fact, on one occasion when it was attempted to hold maximum turbojet rpm during a climb, an over-speed resulted; because it was very violent, a complete disassembly and inspection of the turbojet engine was required.

The decision to air-launch the Skyrocket was a natural one, to be sure. It had been disconcerting to watch the ease at which the Bell X-1 was being handled. No takeoff struggles [the X-1 did make one ground takeoff; it was performed by Chuck Yeager, naturally!], no climb-out and flight to altitude just to carry a minimal supply of rocket motor fuel only to have to fight the performance of the turbojet engine and to guard against its flame-out during the accelerated speed and/or altitude run. So with US Navy approval it was decided to prepare two of the three Skyrockets that had been built for aerial launches. One Skyrocket only, however, was to have its turbojet engine removed, and in its place, additional rocket motor fuel was to be carried. The other air-launched Skyrocket was to keep its turbojet-engine/rocket-motor combination for other flight-test purposes.

My first air-launched flight in the rocket-only Skyrocket came after some eight unsuccessful attempts were made. Climbing to launch altitude in the B-29, piloted by George R. Jansen [a US Air Force pilot who later became a test pilot for Douglas], I polished the gold fish bowl [tinted face plate on the helmet] I would soon be wearing. Just before launch altitude was reached, two of the launch crewmen helped lower down and into the air vehicle. While they closed the cockpit canopy, I plugged in the plane's oxygen hose to my face mask. Some 5min before drop, Jansen gave notice on the B-29's communication system. The chase pilot, flying an F-86, moved in close on the starboard side as I charged the Skyrocket's propulsion system. If the on-board gauges read normal, we moved up to the 1min warning as the cockpit was being pressurized. I flipped on the data switch that started the on-board cameras and the all-important flight instrumentation that would record the aircraft's flight parameters throughout the event. Usually about this time I began to wish very much that I had taken Mother's advice and had actually attended dental school instead. But by now it was 10sec to go and George [Jansen] was busy counting them off: 10. . .9. . .8. . . 7. . . 6, and down. The holding shackles were released, and, like some kind of a large bomb, I was duly dropped.

After the drop, some 100ft below and behind the B-29, I fired the number-one chamber. When the fuel system pressures came up to their correct readings, I fired the trio of remaining chambers as fast as I could flip their switches.

The plane had been dropped out of the B-29's belly at a speed that was slow for her. She is very heavy at this stage, and at first, even though all four chambers of the rocket motor had been fired-off, she seemed motionless and her subsequent acceleration is not very fast. Regardless, to stay out of an accelerated-stall situation, I had to initiate the climb immediately. Her climb at first was more than a little disappointing. The pitch-up angle of the nose is too steep to see the ground and make any references. But one look at the altimeter did convince me of the phenomenal climb rate I was experiencing. At first we had a standard altimeter in the cockpit but found it

advisable to remove the needle that measured 100ft increments as it revolved. The reason: the climb rate had become so fast that the needle had become a blur.

Suddenly, since the 100ft increment needle was neither in the gauge nor wanted, I found myself shooting past the altitude predetermined as optimum for the pushover point and maneuver. When I initiated the pushover maneuver, I hung on for a few seconds to enjoy what can only be described as a ride that was very interesting. For I was experiencing weightlessness!

Then quite suddenly the airplane seemed to buck a couple of times, and I realized, "that's all she wrote." The fuel for the rocket motor is gone and the powered part of the flight is over. Now she's an unpowered glider and she needs to get back to terra firma. She definitely doesn't want to turn at these reduced speeds, but by taking what are sometimes drastic actions [pitching the nose straight down for example], I can trick her into turning to where I want to go. She continues to slow up as I keep concentrating on my long coast home and, hopefully, a good, safe dead-stick landing.

During a later flight, as I banked the plane downwind for landing, I noticed the landing gear indicator was unsafe. Chuck Yeager was flying chase in an F-86 and I asked him to look over the landing gear. He slid his F-86 under me and disappeared from my view. He then requested I retract the gear, which I did. I felt a little bump. And over the radio I heard an unkind word. He added in somewhat of an unfriendly tone of voice, "O.K., let's try it again. Only this time give me a chance to get my head out of the wheel well before you yank the gear handle!" It worked and he slid his F-86 out from under my ride about the very same time I leveled off for landing.

So, a typical air-launched rocket-powered flight to sonic speed as was carried out by Douglas Aircraft and myself in preparation for the follow-on Skyrocket flight-test action to be carried out by the NACA [now NASA].

This story by Mr. Bridgeman is derived from two of his speeches, the first presented at the Washington, D.C., section of the Institute of Aeronautical Sciences, 2 October 1951; the second presented to the Society of Automotive Engineers, New York, New York, 12 March 1952. The latter speech was simply called "Some Notes on the Skyrocket." Mr. Bridgeman, a naval aviator before he joined Douglas Aircraft, was a respected test pilot. Bridgeman was the only Douglas test pilot to fly the Douglas X-3 Stiletto (twenty-five out of a total of fifty-one flights, the others being flown by US Air Force and NASA pilots). He enjoyed flying the Skyrocket in which he realized a bit of fame. For on 15 August 1951 he reached a maximum altitude of 74,494ft. Earlier, on 7 August 1951, he attained a maximum speed of 1,250mph (Mach number 1.88). Thus, for a short time, he was called the "world's fastest and highest flying human." But tragically, while on a vacation, he died in the crash of a Grumman Goose while flying between Los Angeles and Catalina Island. In a terrible irony, then, after tempting fate in a less-than-desirable-performing X-3 and an "on the edge" Skyrocket, Bridgeman lost his life in a time-proved airplane that was flying a mere 250mph at only some 10,000ft. One can understand why, when his friends and admirers heard of his death, they just looked downward and shook their heads.

Chapter 2

The Rocket Age: the 1960s

Although the so-called rocket age had essentially begun in the 1940s and 1950s, it really was not known as such until the 1960s when man first attained speeds above four, five, and six times the speed of sound in an airplane; first orbited the earth in manned space capsules; and, toward the end of the 1960s, traveled from the earth to the moon, landed on the moon, walked on the moon, and safely returned to the earth.

Beginning in the late 1940s and culminating in the late 1950s, the Bell X-1, Bell X-2, and Douglas D-558-2 Skyrocket aircraft posted amazing speed and altitude marks which set the stage for the

Created with Air Force funds to train potential astronauts on the skills of piloting an air vehicle in a weightless environment, three Lockheed NF-104A Starfighters were delivered in 1963 to the US Air Force Aerospace Research Pilot School (now US Air Force Test Pilot School) at Edwards AFB. Using one tail-mounted 6,000lb-thrust rocket motor, in addition to one General electric J79 turbojet engine equipped with an afterburner, the three NF-104s were optimized for zoom-climbs to more than 120,000ft before returning to Rogers Dry Lake. Having one already hit an altitude of 118,860ft above Edwards, US Air Force Maj. Robert W. Smith zoom-climbed his NF-104A to 120,800ft on 6 December 1963. Before they were retired from flight status, the trio of NF-104s flew 126 flights in which, for a short time going over the top, potential astronauts experienced weightlessness. The third example survived and is on display next to the US Air Force Test Pilot School; numbers one and two were lost. Shown is the number-one NF-104A zoom-climbing up and away from Edwards AFB in mid-1963. *AFFTC/HO*

North American X-15. This trio moved supersonic flight from 700mph (Mach number 1.06) to 2,094mph (Mach number 3.19) and upped high-altitude flight from 50,000ft to 125,900ft throughout their respective flight-test careers. But it would be the X-15s performances during the 1960s (ending 24 October 1968) that would shatter speed and altitude records by leaps and bounds. Indeed, before the trio of X-15s were finished, Mach numbers 4, 5, and 6 had been attained and surpassed. In addition, altitudes of 150,000ft, 200,000ft, 250,000ft, 300,000ft, and 350,000ft had been reached and exceeded. And out of the twelve men that flew the X-15s in the 1960s, most earned astronaut wings with flights of up to (264,000ft) or higher. The maximum speed and altitude marks of the X-15 are 4,520mph (Mach number 6.70) and 354,200ft. These unofficial world records have not been broken, nor are they likely to be broken by any other plane. They are unofficial records because the X-15 did not takeoff from a runway, but was air-launched by a carrier airplane. Nonetheless, whether ground- or air-launched, no other aircraft has surpassed the awesome performances of the X-15—which in many ways, led the way to six successful moon explorations by twelve US astronauts.

But it was not only the X-15 that excelled at Edwards in the 1960s.

By the end of the 1960s a variable-geometry swing-wing tactical fighter—the General Dynamics F-111, had been fully tested at Edwards and put into service with the US Air Force. And, amazing-

First reaching powered flight status in the early 1960s, the trio of North American X-15s began to turn heads around the world with their awesome speed and altitude marks. In fact, by the end of 1960, the first and second examples had reached a top speed of 2,196mph (Mach number 3.31) and a maximum altitude of 108,997ft. Without number three having even flown yet, the X-15s had flown higher and faster than any other manned airplane ever had, and at the time they had only completed thirty-one of 199 total flights. Long before its extensive modification to the one-of-a-kind X-15A-2, the number-two X-15 is shown, circa mid-1960, just after its launch from a B-52 mother plane. About 90sec after this photograph was snapped from a chase plane, this X-15 could be in near space while romping at more than three times the speed of sound. Before the X-15 program ended, they had flown at 4,520mph (Mach number 6.70) at more than 350,000ft. *Rockwell*

The sixth production Boeing B-52G Stratofortress flies near Edwards in mid-1962 with four (two under each wing) Douglas GAM-87 Skybolt air-launched ballistic missiles. Developed under Weapon System 130, the two-stage Skybolt, with a nuclear warhead, was to be carried by B-52Hs of the US Strategic Air Command and A. V. Roe Vulcans of the British Royal Air Force. The former was to carry four Skybolts, and the latter was to carry two Skybolts. However, on 31 December 1962, even after successful test firings with no failures, the Skybolt program was canceled. This B-52G was used as a compatibility test-bed for the GAM-87 because the B-52H at the time had just entered flight-test operations at Boeing's Wichita, Oklahoma, facility. The B-52G itself being fully optimized to carry two (one under each wing) North American GAM-77 Hound Dog missiles, developed under Weapon System 132. Because of politics and budget cuts, the promising GAM-87 Skybolt program was terminated. *Boeing*

ly, a very large and very heavy six-engine bomber —the North American B-70—had exceeded 2,000mph (Mach number 3) at altitudes above 70,000ft. Too, a large all-missile-armed twin-jet interceptor—the Lockheed F-12—had likewise surpassed Mach number 3 and had exceeded an altitude of 80,000ft. Finally, with other types of aircraft such as the Convair B-58 (which set a world payload-to-altitude record), the NASA M2-F1 (which pioneered wingless lifting-body flight), and the Martin-Marietta X-24A (first of the powered lifting bodies), Edwards remained exciting.

The rocket age in the 1960s then, having followed the jet age of the 1940s and 1950s, only solidified the importance of the first-class flight-test base called Edwards. But in the 1970s to follow, with the advent of fly-by-wire and fly-by-light flight-control systems and the success of the wingless lifting bodies, the space shuttle was made possible.

The NASA-designed and built M2-F1 wingless lifting body air vehicle passes over a portion of Edwards during one of its more than 100 unpowered glide flights at NASA's DFRF from August 1963 to August 1964. The engineless vehicle, nicknamed the "Flying Bathtub" for obvious reasons, is built of plywood over a tubular steel frame. It pioneered the NASA concept of maneuverable flight without conventional wings. First to fly the M2-F1 was NASA pilot Milton O. "Milt" Thompson. It was first tested while being towed behind a car on Rogers Dry Lake. Later, it was towed into the air behind a NASA C-47 to altitudes of about 10,000ft for glide flights back to the lake bed. The subsequent fleet of heavyweight (the M2-F1 was a lightweight), powered wingless lifting bodies were flown from 1966 to 1975 and helped in the development of the space shuttles. *NASA*

Prior to the flight-test phases of the two North American XB-70A Valkyrie research aircraft, the company had to validate the operation of the crew's emergency escape system—which, in practice, incorporated clam-shell-type ejection capsules, as shown with North American XB-70A chief test pilot Alvin S. "Al" White in early 1964 during a test of the system at Edwards. Unfortunately, in mid-1966, he was forced to use the system for real. On 8 June, a NASA F-104 Starfighter piloted by NASA research pilot Joe Walker had a mid-air collision with the number-two XB-70A. Walker's F-104 exploded on impact and he was killed. The XB-70A, with White as pilot and US Air Force Maj. Carl A. Cross as copilot, lost both of its vertical tails. Cross did not eject from the falling airplane and was killed. White was able to eject, but was severely injured. *Rockwell*

NASA pilot Neil A. Armstrong at the DFRF at Edwards checks out the propulsion unit and engine exhaust gimbaling system of the first of two Lunar Landing Research Vehicles (LLRV) prior to a liftoff and touchdown. The LLRVs were tested from 1964 to 1966 to develop a piloting and procedures program to train Apollo astronauts for lunar landings and takeoffs. The two LLRVs, built by the Bell Aerospace Textron organization in Buffalo, New York, were flown to study controls, pilot displays, visibility, propulsion control, and flight dynamics on a vehicle that could simulate flight in an Apollo lunar module. Its propulsion system was one 4,200lb-thrust turbofan jet engine with a gimbaling engine exhaust nozzle for vehicle control. Additional vehicle control came from a series of hydrogen peroxide rockets. It was these two odd-looking LLRVs that helped make all six moon landings and takeoffs the successes they were. *NASA*

The Paper Clip Flight

by Col. Joseph F. "Joe" Cotton, US Air Force (Retired)

On 30 April 1966 pilot Alvin S. "Al" White [XB-70A chief test pilot for North American Aviation] and myself [XB-70A test director for the US Air Force] as copilot were to take the second of two XB-70A Valkyrie airplanes up for an assault on Mach number 3.0, during which we were to fly over eight western states [California, Oregon, Idaho, Montana, Wyoming, Utah, Nevada and Arizona] in about 30min. This was the thirty-seventh flight-test of XB-70A number two and the thirtieth time we had piloted one of the two air vehicles together.

Using 9,300ft of runway at a take-off weight of 530,000lb, we rotated at 202 knots indicated airspeed to become airborne. About 16sec after lift-off I raised the handle to retract the landing gear. About 5–7sec after raising the handle we heard a muffled *bang* and felt a *thump* in the airframe. I put the landing gear handle down. The main gear indicators were green, the nose gear green light was out, and the red light was illuminated in the gear handle. Maj. William J. "Pete" Knight in a T-38 chase plane reported the nose gear door had not opened far enough and when the nose gear retracted the door jammed between the two nose gear wheels. He reported that the nose gear was about halfway retracted and the left nose gear tire had blown.

As we orbited Edwards at a speed of 225 KIAS and an altitude of 9,000ft, Lt. Col. Fitzhugh L. "Fitz" Fulton [US Air Force] and Van H. "Shep" Shepard [North American Aviation], both assigned to the XB-70A flight-test program, moved in closer with a chase TB-58A and reported both main gear doors open; both bogies in their proper nose-up position.

The hydraulic landing gear sequence of operation called for the doors [closed with gear extended] to open for gear retraction and then trigger an electrical switch to raise the gear. The nose gear door had failed to open fully and the switch had not been triggered in a proper sequence. And even though the nose gear had been prompted to raise, the air pressure jammed its dual wheels up against the partially open door, blowing the left-hand tire with explosive force. Thus the *bang* and *thump*.

Since the nose gear was jammed against the door, there was no way to retract it nor extend it. Knowing this, if a cure couldn't be found, we knew we would have to prepare for an emergency ejection from the air vehicle after heading it for a remote gunnery range—and its crash to destruction, for the airplanes configuration simply would not allow for a landing without its nose gear down and locked. The nose gear, if not down and locked, would collapse upon touchdown, and the XB-70A, with its very long nose, would break up.

We were now forced to circle Edwards while some North American engineers on the ground—Hal Smith and Bob MacDonald, hydraulic engineers; Don Bickhart, electrical engineer; Frank Munds, flight-test controller; and Walt Spivak, chief engineer—worked frantically to find a cure.

While we waited for a plan to be devised on the ground, I moved the landing gear emergency extend switch from *Normal* to *All Gear Down*. The nose gear moved down about 3in and stopped, again indicating to the chase pilots that the nose gear door was the culprit. The main gear doors remained in place. I raised the canard foreplane flaps. When our speed increased to 285 KIAS, Al yawed the airplane out to 4deg left. There was no change. I returned the landing gear emergency extend switch to *Normal*, and the nose gear moved up about 6in. I moved the same switch down again, and again, the nose gear came down 3in. Al yawed right 3deg. This, too, was ineffective. Nothing we tried seemed to work. We began to wonder if we'd be staying with the $500-million-plus airplane much longer.

Working with electrical circuitry diagrams, the engineers on the ground did in fact find a solution to our difficulty. They concluded that two very small pin terminals—among fifteen in a small relay unit in the planes electronics bay—could be cross-circuited to *fool* the nose gear relay switch to extend the nose gear. But we didn't have their electrical diagrams.

I was told to go aft in the plane to the electronics bay and to open the relay unit panel so that I could draw a rough diagram of the relay unit and take it back to the cockpit. It was dark back there—without my flashlight (loaded with fresh Eveready batteries), I couldn't have pulled this off.

Lengthy radio conversations with the engineers on the ground ensued. After checks and re-checks, we, Al and myself, were convinced we knew which two pin terminals to jump across. We had to figure out just how we were going to do that in a safe way. For the idea of jumping anything electrical isn't very popular with most of us.

continued on next page

Joe Cotton (left) and Al White (right).

I thought about using a paper clip as a jumper wire between the two close proximity pin terminals only about 1/3in apart. Al and the engineers on the ground agreed. But I still had to insulate myself from shock. After some thought I decided to cut out a piece of seat belt and use it with a pair of pliers to grip the clip. Being nylon-based, the piece of safety belt would serve as a good insulator. At least I hoped so.

Holding my breath, I simultaneously touched the paper clip—which I had reshaped into the rough shape of a horse shoe—to the terminals.

Al lowered the gear handle and then came the words from the chase pilots: "Gear coming down!" After I returned to the cockpit I saw three green lights indicating that all gears were down and locked. Those three greens looked like a beautiful Christmas tree.

Our next problem was landing. Could the big airplane, still weighing some 307,000lb, be landed safely at almost 175 KIAS with one of its nose gear wheels flat? Could it be controlled on the landing roll?

A master pilot, Al decided to save enough fuel [not to dump most of it as is standard procedure during emergency landings] to land sufficiently fast enough to take-off again if it appeared the blown-out tire was going to make the plane unmanageable upon nose-gear touch-down.

At the time we didn't know the malfunction had also locked six of the eight wheels on the main landing-gear assemblies. That, in itself, made it a bail-out situation. Not only was one of the nose-gear wheels flat, but we would land and roll-out to a stop with only three out of ten wheels turning. Now that I'm recalling the situation, I'm glad we didn't know about it.

With a great deal of finesse, Al landed the airplane. As soon as the nose gear touched-down, according to our chase pilots, the main gear burst into flames. And during the entire length of our 7,000ft slide to a stop, the nose of the plane shook violently from side-to-side from the drag induced by seven non-rotating wheels and airless tires. The shake was so bad that the airplane's nose boom skipped around and broke.

Fortunately, even though we had landed at 172 KIAS [258mph], the airplane stayed relatively straight during the roll-out until it had nearly came to a full stop, when it did veer to the right a bit. It had been 2hr and 16min since we had lifted-off.

Damage to the airplane was mild, and on 16 May we took it back up for a check flight, which culminated with a speed run of Mach number 2.73 at 65,000ft. Three days later, we got to accomplish our goal of two earlier flights—that is, we flew over those eight western states at a continuous speed of Mach number 3.0 for 32min at 72,500ft.

But going back to the paper clip flight, personally, I feel what could have been a real disaster had been diverted by a group of engineers and two pilots who had, for the most part, "grown-up" with the airplane—first, as a weapon system, and lastly, as a high-speed, high-altitude research airplane.

As an aside, through my own experience, it had become second nature for me to carry along a tool kit on test flights. In the kit I found all the tools I needed to apply corrective action within the pin-terminal panel—that is, a flashlight with fresh batteries (it allowed me to see what I was doing), a pair of pliers, a slot-type screw driver, and a pair of diagonal cutters. The all-important paper clip, a five-and-dime-store item, was holding together a 1/2in-thick stack of flight-log papers.

When the XB-70A flight-test program ended on 4 February 1969, Joe Cotton had flown as pilot nineteen times, copilot for forty-three times; Al White had flown as pilot forty-nine times, copilot for eighteen times.

XB-70A flight-test pilots Fulton and Shepard, the TB-58A chase plane crew during the Paper Clip Flight, respectively piloted the aircraft thirty-one and twenty-three times; copiloted the aircraft thirty-two and twenty-three times.

First flown on 7 August 1963 at Nellis AFB, Nevada, with Lockheed test pilot James D. "Jim" Eastham at the stick, the first of three Lockheed YF-12As (shown) and two others were soon undergoing flight-test and armament-test activities at Edwards AFB. The two-place YF-12A has a wingspan of 55ft 7in, a length of 101ft 8in, a height of 18ft 3in, and a gross weight of 127,000lb. Powered by two afterburning 34,000lb-thrust-class Pratt & Whitney J58 dual-cycle turbojet engines, the YF-12A had a top speed of 2,200mph (Mach number 3.35) at more than 80,000ft. The YF-12 was proposed as an all-weather manned interceptor to be armed with four Hughes AIM-47 air-to-air guided missiles (one is shown). The YF-12A, top secret until its public debut at Edwards on 30 September 1964, featured the advanced Hughes pulse-Doppler AN/ASG-18 radar and fire-control system. It was the second in the series of Lockheed Blackbird air vehicles—the A-12 and SR-71 being the first and third types respectively. *USAF via Tony Landis*

Following its third flight, the number-one North American XB-70A Valkyrie returned to Palmdale for additional static tests. That fourth flight on 24 October 1964, like the first three flights, were with Al White as pilot, and Joseph F. "Joe" Cotton as copilot. On 16 February 1965, after the static tests were complete, the same men returned the airplane to Edwards. The XB-70As accumulated 129 flights (eighty-three for number one; forty-six for number two) from 21 September 1964 to 4 February 1969. Originally proposed as a Boeing B-52 Stratofortress supplement and replacement, the B-70, as a bomber, was canceled. Instead, to investigate triplesonic speed and other parameters associated with large aircraft, the "Triplesonic Twosome," as they were called, became research aircraft for the Air Force and NASA. *Rockwell*

The Lockheed YF-12A set a number of world's absolute Class C, Group III records on 1 May 1965, while assigned to the 4786th Test Squadron at Edwards AFB. These included a sustained altitude flight of 80,258ft, a speed of 2,070.102mph (Mach number 3.27) over a closed-circuit course measuring 15 by 25km (9.3mi by 15.5mi), and a speed of 1,643.042mph (Mach number 2.48) over a 500km (310mi) closed-circuit course. Lockheed had hoped that its three YF-12As (number three is shown) would lead to a production order for its proposed F-12B, which—as proved by YF-12A missile firings—could have destroyed aircraft more than 100mi from missile launch point. The YF-12A's twin vertical tails, made from plastic and canted inward, and the chines on the outboard side of the engine nacelles and on the sides of the fuselage helped to reduce the aircraft's radar cross-section in an early attempt at stealth. *Lockheed*

Beginning on 2 May 1965—following the arrival of the second of eighteen full-scale-development General Dynamics F-111 aircraft, an intense flight-test program for the type was initiated at Edwards. Developed under the Tactical Fighter, Experimental or TFX program, whereby one airplane was to suit the Air Force, Navy, and Marine Corps, the first batch of Γ-111A aircraft were powered by two afterburning 18,000lb-thrust-class Pratt & Whitney TF30-P-1 turbofan jet engines. Production F-111s had a top speed of more than 1,750mph (Mach number 2.5) and feature the use of the world's first practical variable-geometry swing-wing; it is unswept for takeoffs, landings, and low-speed flight and swept-back for high-speed flight. The original F-111A has a wingspan of 63ft unswept (31ft 11-1/2in swept), a length of 73ft 5-1/2in, a height of 17ft 6in, and a gross weight of 82,800lb. Originally armed with two AIM-9 Sidewinders and one AGM-12 Bullpup carried within its internal weapons bay, later F-111s carry a wide variety of tactical ordnance, both conventional and nuclear, for air-to-air and air-to-ground warfare. The Navy/Marine version was never ordered into production. The Air Force, however, ordered a number of versions including the FB-111, optimized as a strategic bomber. The numbers six and twelve full-scale-development F-111As are shown during their ferry flights to Edwards in late 1965. *General Dynamics*

Thoughts On The XB-70A Valkyrie

Lt. Col. Fitzhugh L. "Fitz" Fulton, Jr.,
US Air Force (Retired)

The XB-70A Valkyrie, built by North American Aviation (now the aircraft division of Rockwell International Corporation) under contract to the US Air Force, is the only very large plane (fueled, it weighed much more than 500,000lb) to be built that could fly more than three times the speed of sound (2,000mph). Originally designed as a dedicated weapon system, the plane was flown only to obtain research data and provided much valuable information during the US Air Force test program and later during the NASA test program.

I was privileged to be part of the original team of four test pilots who were assigned to the program long before the first flight in September 1964. That pilot team was Al White and Van Shepard of North American Aviation and Col. Joe Cotton and myself of the US Air Force. When NASA took over on the XB-70A test program in 1967, I joined NASA and became the NASA chief project pilot on the air vehicle.

The Valkyrie was a unique airplane. It is very large; it has beautiful lines and it is constructed primarily of stainless steel. The data gathered during its test programs has provided a vast pool of knowledge that has been used and is still being used in the design of other aircraft. The outstanding Rockwell B-1B Lancer bomber has many design features that were first tried on the XB-70A. It only takes a quick look into the B-1B cockpit to see a few of them.

The XB-70A was designed and manufactured by an outstanding team of people. The US Air Force, NASA, and many contractor flight-test teams were just as outstanding. The top quality people on the program is one of the things that stand out in my mind when I think back about the project.

The XB-70A was not a particularly difficult airplane for experienced test pilots to fly. It was, however, an airplane that had different systems and different flying characteristics than any other airplane. The pilots had to be very knowledgeable about the airplane and prepared to handle any emergencies if and when they occurred [witness "The Paper Clip Flight"]. Even though it was a very large and heavy airplane, the two pilots were the only people on board. Engineers and technicians in the control room could, and often did, provide valuable information by radio, but the pilots had to make the final decisions and solve the problems.

There were many highlights and emotional highs on the program as things were done for the first time and when major milestones were accomplished. There were also some very sad times, as when two of the ground crew were seriously hurt during a fueling operation. Both were to eventually die from their injuries. It was also a very sad day then the number-two XB-70A was lost after a mid-air collision on 8 June 1966. Its copilot, Maj. Carl Cross, on his first XB-70A flight, was killed along with NASA test pilot Joe Walker in the escort airplane; its pilot Al White, though injured, survived.

A total of 129 test missions were flown on the two XB-70A air vehicles. The final flight-test phase on the program was conducted by NASA between early 1967 and February 1969. Don Mallick of NASA and US Air Force Col. Ted Sturmthal joined me as the pilots of the number-one XB-70A during that series of flights. I flew as pilot on the last flight of the last surviving XB-70A from Edwards AFB to the Air Force Museum at Dayton, Ohio; that was 4 February 1969. Ted Sturmthal was copilot and Don Mallick flew along side in the B-58 escort airplane. The air vehicle—the largest and heaviest to ever fly at three times the speed of sound, is on permanent display there.

Fitz Fulton, for all his aerospace-related accomplishments through more than four decades, has for the most part been ignored. But this is partially due to his quiet and humble nature. Never really wanting his "name in lights," Mr. Fulton is a true gentleman and a credit to his US Air Force and NASA flight-test-pilot peers. Having served in the US Air Force for twenty-two years, he joined NASA to serve yet another twenty years. Fulton, during his two full careers, has flown everything from the T-6 Texan to the SR-71 Blackbird. Whether a single-engine or a multi-engine airplane, a piston-powered, propeller-driven or turbojet-powered airplane, there was no difference. He just flew them.

Fitz Fulton.

The main mission of the North American B-70 Valkyrie was that of an intercontinental strategic bomber capable of carrying up to 50,000lb of nuclear bombs. Designed to attain constant triplesonic speed (2,000mph), production Valkyries were to be powered by various versions of the afterburning General Electric J93 turbojet engine. But after the B-70 bomber was canceled because of politics and budget cuts, the two prototype XB-70As appeared with service-test YJ93-GE-3 engines—six each, developing more than 30,000lb of thrust with continuous afterburning. During flight-test, the number-two XB-70A attained a top speed of 1,950mph (Mach number 3.08) on 12 April 1966; it had earlier reached a peak altitude of 74,000ft. The two-place XB-70A (production B-70s would have been four-place) has a wingspan of 105ft, a length of 189ft (196ft with the instrumented nose boom), a height of 30ft, and a gross weight of 550,000lb. It was to fly 7,600nm (unrefueled) at 2,175mph (Mach number 3.20) and 95,000ft. The XB-70's fold-down wing tips and a splitter plate between its engine air inlets allowed it to ride atop its own supersonic shock waves, taking advantage of a NASA discovery, *compression lift,* to greatly increase its lift-to-drag ratio. The number-one air vehicle, on its last flight on 4 February 1969, was delivered to the US Air Force Museum at Dayton, Ohio. Number two is shown following its 1,950mph (Mach number 3.08) flight. *Rockwell*

An extremely rare photograph of the NASA F-104 flying in formation with the number-two XB-70A just prior to the mid-air collision between them on 8 June 1966. Tragically, just moments after this photo was taken, the F-104, piloted Joe Walker, collided with the XB-70A. The F-104 rolled over the top of the XB-70A inverted and sheared off both of its vertical tails, and the Starfighter and the Valkyrie fell to the desert floor below. Joe Walker and Maj. Carl S. Cross (copilot of the XB-70A) were killed. Al White (pilot of the ill-fated XB-70A) survived. No one actually knows why Walker's F-104 raised upward and collided with the right wing tip of the doomed XB-70A. *USAF via Tom Rosquin*

Following its last flight on 3 October 1967 when Capt. William J. Knight (having sixteen X-15 flights) took it out to 102,100ft and 4,520mph (Mach number 6.70), the modified number-two X-15A-2 was retired. Shown with the number-one XB-70A at the DFRF in early 1968, this particular X-15 was the fastest of the three built; number three at 354,200ft, was the highest flying. Air-launched, the X-15A-2 has a wingspan of 22ft 3in, a length of 52ft 4-1/2in, a height of 12ft 1in, and a gross (launch) weight of 56,130lb. Having flown at 4,520mph (Mach number 6.70) its current speed is zero at the US Air Force Museum, Dayton, Ohio. The number-one X-15 is on permanent display at the National Air and Space Museum, Washington, D.C. The number-three X-15 disintegrated at 3,480mph (Mach number 5.0) and 125,000ft on 15 November 1967 killing its pilot, Maj. Michael J. Adams. The X-15 program, still hailed as one of aviation's most rewarding flight-test activities (their data is still being evaluated), lasted from 8 June 1959 to 24 October 1968. It was the first airplane to exceed Mach numbers 4, 5, and 6—and it was the first airplane to exceed altitudes of 100,000ft, 200,000ft, and 300,000ft. Much bigger and heavier, taking-off under its own power, the XB-70A parked behind the X-15A-2, amazingly went half as fast. *NASA*

The Northrop HL-10 wingless lifting body hangs from the right wing pylon mount of a NASA B-52 as the mated pair climb up and away from Rogers Dry Lake for another flight of the small research craft that helped lead the way to America's successful fleet of space shuttles. The HL-10—fastest and highest flying of the lifting bodies—was one of seven lifting bodies flown by NASA's DFRF from July 1966 to November 1976 in a program to study and validate the concept of maneuvering and safely landing a low-lift-to-drag ratio air vehicle designed for reentry from space. *NASA*

Chapter 3

The Lifting Bodies: the 1970s

After the X-15 program, the US Air Force and the NASA partnership turned to different kinds of experimental rocket-powered air vehicles—that is, specially shaped, wingless air vehicles called lifting bodies. Not designed for speeds and altitudes reached by the X-15s, the lifting bodies were shaped to fly both as spacecraft and as wingless aircraft. They were tested to determine the qualities for an extended near-earth flight and for conventional runway approach and landing maneuvers. The knowledge gained from the lifting body research aided in the development of the reusable space shuttle fleet, which carries personnel and equipment to space, returning to earth by landing on the ground like an airplane. The space shuttle helps to eliminate costly "throw-away" boosters and ocean splashdowns. With one exception, all the lifting bodies were carried aloft underneath the wing of a Boeing B-52 Stratofortress mother ship and then released to perform their flight-test activities.

The exception was the M2-F1 "Flying Bath-tub" which was towed by a Douglas C-47 Skytrain to an altitude of 12,000 ft and released. Its successors, however, the M2-F2 and M2-F3, were dropped from the B-52.

As a follow-on to the NASA M2-F1 and Martin-Marietta X-23A lifting bodies, having first flown on 2 September 1963 and 17 April 1969, respectively, it was time to wring-out the third type of lifting body—the Northrop HL-10, which had made its first flight on 22 December 1966. The HL-10 made thirty-seven flights, twenty-two of which were powered.

So as the 1970s began, on 18 February 1970, the HL-10 hit 1,200mph (Mach number 1.86) which turned out to be the highest speed ever attained by a lifting-body air vehicle. It was piloted by US Air Force test pilot Maj. Pete Hoag. Nine days later on 27 February, NASA test pilot Bill Dana flew the HL-10 to 90,303ft, the highest altitude ever reached by a lifting body.

The US Air Force X-24A lifting body, built by Martin-Marietta, had made its aerial debut at Edwards in a glide flight on 17 April 1969, almost a year before Hoag's and Dana's HL-10 flights. Before the X-24A was retired, US Air Force and NASA test pilots flew the unique air vehicle twenty-eight times, including seventeen rocket-powered flights.

The X-24A's airframe was modified into the much more refined X-24B configuration. The X-24B's first flight was conducted at Edwards on 1 August 1973, and during the thirty-six test flights that followed it became the first lifting body to

Following its thirty-sixth and last flight on 26 November 1975 (piloted by NASA pilot Thomas McMurtry), the one-of-a-kind Martin-Marietta X-24B descends to a landing on Rogers Dry Lake at Edwards. The wingless, tri-tailed X-24B lifting body made its first flight (unpowered glide flight) on 1 August 1973, piloted by NASA's John Manke. Rocket-powered, its best speed and altitude marks were 1,155mph (Mach number 1.76) and 74,130ft respectively. *NASA*

land on a concrete runway. Previous flights had ended with landings on the dry lake bed. Lifting-body research was completed on 26 November 1975 when the X-24B made its final flight.

But it was not just the lifting-body aircraft that made news in the 1970s at Edwards. Before the decade was over two new attack aircraft—the Northrop YA-9A and the Republic YA-10A—were tested; three new fighter planes—the McDonnell Douglas F-15, General Dynamics F-16, and the Northrop F-17—had been tested; two new transport types—the Boeing YC-14 and McDonnell Douglas YC-15—were evaluated; and, the first space shuttle—the non-orbital *Enterprise*,—had made five successful Approach and Landing Test (ALT) glide flights. It was a busy decade filled with many new advancements which, in the 1980s, would be put into practice on a concurrent basis.

Two of the experimental aircraft flown at Edwards were NASA's F-8C DFBW (Digital Fly-By-Wire), shown in the foreground, and the F-8A SCW (supercritical wing). The two airplanes were flown extensively to test two advanced aeronautical concepts. The F-8C DFBW airplane tested a flight-control scheme that used an electronic system coupled to a digital computer instead of conventional mechanical flight controls. This led to today's common use of fly-by-wire flight-control systems found on aircraft such as the F-16 and F-117. The F-8A SCW airplane evaluated in flight a new airfoil shape that reduced the operating costs of aircraft by permitting them to cruise at higher speeds while using less power and less fuel. Now retired and displayed side-by-side at the DFRF, both aircraft were extensively tested during the 1970s. *NASA*

First flown on 27 July 1972 with McDonnell Douglas test pilot Irving L. "Irv" Burrows, Jr., at the controls, the first F-15 Eagle streaks along near Edwards. Developed under the Air Force's FX program to find a new breed of air-superiority fighter, the F-15, initially powered by two afterburning 25,000lb-thrust-class Pratt & Whitney F100-PW-100 turbofan jet engines, became the first fighter in the world to develop more pounds of powerplant thrust than airframe weight. Thus, in a vertical climb, it could fly at supersonic speed! The original F-15 had a wingspan of 42ft 9-3/4in, a length of 63ft 9-3/4in, a height of 18ft, 7-1/2in, and a gross weight of 41,500lb. Capable of speeds greater than 1,660mph (Mach number 2.5), production F-15As have a primary armament of four AIM-7 Sparrow and four AIM-9 Sidewinder air-to-air guided missiles and one 20mm multi-barrel rotary cannon. Though twin vertical tails are now common on fighters, it was the F-15 that first featured such a configuration in the United States. Arguably, the best air-to-air combat fighter-interceptor in the world today, the F-15's air superiority has begun to fade away. *AFFTC/HO*

First flown at Edwards on 2 February 1974 with General Dynamics test pilot Philip F. "Phil" Oestricher at the controls, the first of two General Dynamics YF-16s made a successful debut while awaiting its Lightweight Fighter (LWF) competition—two Northrop YF-17s. Powered by one afterburning 25,000lb-thrust-class Pratt & Whitney F100-PW-100 turbofan jet engine, the YF-16 posted top speeds of more than 1,385mph (Mach number 2.1) during their flight-test activities. The single-seat YF-16 has a wingspan of 31ft, a length of 46ft 6in, a height of 16ft 3in, and a gross weight of 27,000lb. Ultimately, after winning the LWF fly-off competition, initial production F-16A/Bs came armed with a multi-barrel rotary-action 20mm cannon, two AIM-7 Sparrow guided missiles (one under each wing), and two AIM-9 Sidewinder guided missiles (one on each wing tip). Capable of 9g maneuvers, the F-16, later named Fighting Falcon, has proved itself to be a top-notch air-combat fighter and is also capable of precise air-to-ground weapons delivery. Still in production for the US Air Force and a number of friendly nations some twenty years after its debut, F-16s are now being manufactured by Lockheed at General Dynamics' former Fort Worth, Texas, plant. *General Dynamics*

Powered by two afterburning 15,000lb-thrust-class General Electric YJ101-GE-100 turbojet engines (forerunner of the hallmark General Electric F404 turbofan jet engine), both Northrop YF-17 aircraft fly near Edwards AFB. The first example (foreground), with Northrop test pilot Henry E. "Hank" Chouteau at the controls, made a successful first flight at Edwards on 9 June 1974, and number two made its first flight on 21 August 1974. The YF-17 has a wingspan of 35ft, a length of 56ft, a height of 14ft 6in, and a gross weight of 23,000lb. The second example (background) was later used to evaluate the feasibility of producing a combination fighter and attack version of the type for Navy and Marine Corps operations—and since the YF-17 had lost the LWF competition to the YF-16, it was a perfect candidate for such a program. After Northrop teamed-up with McDonnell Douglas, the YF-17 was redesigned and later emerged as the larger F/A-18 Hornet. Today, the F/A-18 is a major weapons system for both the Navy and the Marine Corps. *AFFTC/HO*

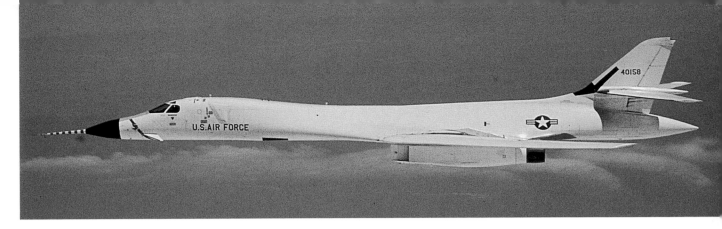

Known only as the Advanced Manned Strategic Aircraft (AMSA) until early 1969, the first of four Rockwell B-1A aircraft made its first flight—Palmdale to Edwards on 23 December 1974. It was flown by Rockwell's Charles C. "Charlie" Bock Jr. (pilot) and Col. Emil "Ted" Sturmthal (copilot); the flight-test engineer was Richard "Dick" Abrams. Production B-1As were to supplement and replace Boeing B-52 Stratofortresses. Powered by four afterburning 30,000lb-thrust-class General Electric YF101-GE-100 turbofan jet engines, the B-1A had a maximum speed of 1,452mph (Mach number 2.2) at 50,000ft. The four-place B-1A features a variable-sweep wing that spans 78ft 2-1/2in (swept) and 136ft 8-1/2in (unswept). The B-1A has a length of 150ft 2-1/2 in with its nose instrumentation probe, a height of 33ft 7-1/4in, and a gross weight of 395,000lb. Production B-1As were to carry up to 50,000lb of weapons—nuclear and conventional—some 6,000mi without refueling. In the late 1970s, after 347 flights and 1,895.2 total hours of flight, the four B-1A aircraft were retired and placed in extended storage. Five years later, however, the B-1A was updated and put into production as the B-1B. *Rockwell*

Following its successful 2hr-plus first flight—Long Beach to Edwards AFB—on 26 August 1975, the first of two service-test McDonnell Douglas YC-15 four-jet AMST (Advanced Medium STOL [short takeoff and landing] Transport) aircraft began an extensive flight-test program at the base. Identically powered by four non-afterburning 16,000lb-thrust Pratt & Whitney JT8D-17 turbofan jet engines, the second YC-15 arrived at Edwards after its first flight in December 1975. The YC-15 has a wingspan of 110ft 4in, a length of 124ft 3in, a height of 43ft 4in, and a fully-loaded gross takeoff weight of 219,180lb. Although the YC-15 performed well, neither it nor its competitor, the Boeing YC-14, were ever ordered into production. The number-two YC-15 is shown. *AFFTC/HO*

Forerunner to the amazing AFTI (Advanced Fighter Technology Integration) F-16 was the Control Configured Vehicle (CCV) F-16, which underwent a 125hr flight-test program (beginning in March 1976) at Edwards to explore fighter CCV technology in eighty-seven flights. The number-one General Dynamics YF-16 prototype aircraft was used. Its analog fly-by-wire flight-control system was modified to provide the "new-way-to-fly" CCV flight modes. Canards under the engine air inlet—one on either side of centerline, like those on the AFTI F-16—were added, and there were changes to the cockpit controls and displays. For increased in-flight control of the aircraft's center-of-gravity, its fuel system was modified. During flight-testing, the YF-16 demonstrated that fighter CCV technology can be effectively used for innovative flight capabilities. The CCV F-16 could shift its flight path laterally or vertically without pitch or roll inputs. Its nose could be pointed up or down without power changes and left or right as it maintained a constant track over the ground. And it could turn without banking. *USAF*

Powered by two non-afterburning 50,000lb-thrust-class General Electric CF6-50D turbofan jet engines, the first of two service-test Boeing YC-14 AMST aircraft flies near Edwards with a Grumman A-6 Intruder and a McDonnell Douglas AV-8B Harrier II tagging along. Having made its first flight on 9 August 1976 at Boeing's Seattle facility, the number-one YC-14 has a wingspan of 129ft, a length of 131ft 8in, a height of 48ft 4in, and with its fully-loaded maximum gross takeoff of 251,000lb, it matched the four-jet McDonnell Douglas YC-15's performance. *AFFTC/HO*

To confirm the low-speed airworthiness of the Space Shuttle, six ALT (approach and landing test) glide flights were scheduled for the late 1970s at Edwards. On 12 August 1977, the Rockwell International-built Space Shuttle *Enterprise* (the only non-orbiting shuttle to be built) was launched from the spine of the NASA 747 Shuttle Carrier Aircraft at 24,100ft—after which, it successfully completed a 5min 21sec descent to a landing and roll-out on Rogers Dry Lake. This first ALT (along with four subsequent ALTs; number six was not required) demonstrated the soundness of the shuttle's aerodynamic design and confirmed the approach and landing techniques that would later be employed by shuttle astronauts returning from space. The first three ALTs were performed with the tail cone attached as shown. The last two ALTs were performed without the tail cone, but with equally good results. Two shuttle crews flew the ALT demonstration flights, which concluded in October 1977. *NASA*

One of the two NASA B-52 air-launch aircraft is shown carrying a Space Shuttle solid-rocket-booster parachute-recovery system test article. This B-52 was used as a test aircraft for four years before it was assigned to NASA as a launch aircraft for the X-15 program. It flew a total of 161 captive-carry and launch flights in the X-15 program and was later used on 128 of the 144 drop flights in the lifting-body program. The airplane—shown here in the late 1970s—most recently supported the Pegasus Air-Launched Space Vehicle program for the ARPA in the early 1990s. *NASA*

Chapter 4

Concurrent Technologies: the 1980s

During the 1980s at Edwards, a number of concurrent technologies were developed. These included the analog and digital computer-generated fly-by-wire and fly-by-light flight-control systems, the supercritical airfoil for wings, the close-coupled canard (foreplane), the forward-swept wing, the oblique wing, the use of composite materials, the mission-adaptive wing, the X-wing, and the investigation of short takeoffs and landings with a highly maneuverable technology demonstrator.

For first testing the analog and digital computer-generated fly-by-wire and fly-by-light flight-control systems, it was the General Dynamics F-16 Fighting Falcon; and the Vought A-7D Corsair 2 respectively. Today, in concert, both types of flight-control systems are used by an ever-growing number of various aircraft types including bombers, fighters, helicopters, and transports.

The supercritical wing, whereby the top of an airfoil is flat and the bottom is curved—just the reverse of a normal wing—was developed and tested by the NASA on a modified F-8A. Now, to gain range with the same amount of fuel at less power and higher speed, supercritical wings are common to all types of modern planes.

The close-coupled canard (foreplane)—first used by the Wright Brothers in 1903,—was dusted off and recently used on the Grumman X-29 Forward-Swept Wing Advanced Technology Demonstrator. Essentially, since a foreplane is positioned ahead of a wing instead of behind it, and using variable-incidence (sixty degrees down, thirty degrees up from the horizontal), it shared the aerodynamic load of the X-29s forward-swept wing; it also provided the X-29s primary pitch (nose-up, nose-down) control.

First used on a German bomber airplane in World War II, the Junkers Ju-287, and later on a German business plane, the HFB-320 Hansajet, the forward-swept wing was unpopular among aircraft designers. The reason: it had a tendency to rip off when an aircraft exceeded 400mph (Mach number 0.74) due to a problem called structural divergence; that is, when a wing encounters too much twist. The X-29, with a forward-swept wing made out of tailored advanced composite materials—providing more strength than conventional

In the 1980s, under a joint NASA/US Air Force program, Rockwell International built two sub-scale Highly Maneuverable Aircraft Technology (HiMAT) or remotely-piloted research vehicles (RPRV) to demonstrate the maneuverability of a 1990s conceptual fighter-type aircraft. The HiMAT RPRVs were carried aloft by a B-52 mother ship and launched at altitude, typically 45,000ft. Powered by afterburning General Electric J85-GE-21 turbojet engines and controlled by a pilot on the ground or in a chase airplane, the HiMATs flew about 25min after release, then landed on Rogers Dry Lake. The 3,400lb RPRVs reached speeds of 925mph at 45,000ft and experienced a maximum load factor of 8g. The HiMAT RPRVs were built to a scale of about 44 percent that of a modern day fighter. Both HiMATs (number two in the foreground) pose on Rogers Dry Lake, circa 1983. *NASA*

wings made of aluminum—proved that modern fighter-types could safely employ such a wing. However, even though the X-29 passed all flight-tests with flying colors, no fighter has yet adopted such a wing planform. One reason, as one X-29 test pilot reported, "I believe that the next generation of fighter aircraft will be dominated in shape by the need for signature control (stealth), and that this requirement will exclude forward-swept wing design. If you look at the distinct shapes of the B-2, F-22 and F-117 you will easily understand what I mean."

The oblique wing, developed and tested by NASA on a NASA designed and built airplane--the AD-1, pivoted fore and aft during flight. In other words, if the right-hand side of the wing pivoted forward, the left-hand side of the wing pivoted aft and vice versa. With those actions, NASA found a low-powered aircraft would perform more like a high-powered aircraft. Moreover, the oblique wing concept offered good low-speed stability and control characteristics without the need of complex high-lift devices.

The use of advanced composite materials in the construction of aircraft is now status quo. Thoroughly tested and Edwards and elsewhere, these materials provide modern aircraft with more structural strength with less structural weight. And, as now revealed, they help military aircraft types such as the B-2 and F-22 avoid detection by enemy radar.

The mission-adaptive wing, tested on a Boeing-modified General Dynamics F-111A, demonstrated automatic leading- and trailing-edge wing

On 24 March 1982, a modified Vought A-7D Corsair II, equipped with an optical fiber as a data link in its DFBW flight-control system under the Digital Tactical Aircraft Control (DIGITAC) program, made its first flight at Edwards. This was the first time that a fiber-optics (FO) subsystem—popularly called fly-by-light—had ever been flown on a US military airplane. The DIGITAC airplane was created from the number-two A-7D, and following twenty additional flights at Edwards, the plane's unique fly-by-light system proved to be extremely reliable. *USAF*

bends without the leading-edge slat and trailing-edge flat splits normally found along the wing. This benefit, if employed on stealthy aircraft, helps to reduce their radar cross-section and thus increase their radar cross-section and thus increase their survivability.

The X-wing configured air vehicle was a specially modified, Sikorsky-built, winged and tailed aerocopter for a joint NASA and ARPA flight-test program that began in August 1986. Oddly, when the X-wing program ended in 1988, the aerocopter had not flown with its unique main rotor attached. The X-wing was to perform as follows: When the main four-bladed rotor (with very wide

rotor blades) was stopped in flight, the blades were to provide aerodynamic lift assistance to the aerocopters stubby wings extending outward from the air vehicles lower fuselage. Although the X-wing never flew with the rotor attached, it did a series of taxi tests with it attached. The reason for this is unclear; however, it is assumed that the advent of the Bell Boeing V-22 Osprey program might be the reason.

The investigation of short takeoffs and landings with a highly maneuverable technology demonstrator in the 1980s continues today with the nothing less than amazing McDonnell Douglas F-15 SMTD (Stol [Short Take Off and Land-

The AFTI F-16 flight-test program—with more than 600 flights already recorded—is being carried out to integrate and demonstrate new technologies for next-generation close-air-support and battlefield-air-interdiction (CAS/BAI) aircraft. The joint NASA, Air Force, Navy and Army AFTI F-16 flight-test program is managed by the Air Force, and flight operations are conducted at NASA's DFRF at Edwards. Early in the AFTI F-16 program, which began in July 1982, the unique airplane had demonstrated voice-activated commands, helmet-mounted sights, flat turns, and selective fuselage pointing using the forward-mounted canards and a triplex DFBW flight-control system. The CAS/BAI phase helped to develop and demonstrate advanced technologies and capabilities to find and destroy ground targets, day or night, and in adverse weather at low altitude. The airplane is equipped with a Maneuvering Terrain Following/Terrain Avoidance/Threat Avoidance system, Forward-Looking Infrared, and sensors that give the pilot a look-into-turn capability. *NASA*

ing] and Maneuver Technology Demonstrator) airplane. With its thrust vectoring and thrust reversing two-dimensional engine exhaust nozzles and canard foreplanes (modified F/A-18 stabilators), this Eagle can take off in 1,000ft or less and land and stop in less than 1,250ft.

It was a decade when two new strategic bomb-ers—the B-1B and B-2A—first appeared; the fleet of US space shuttles—the *Challenger, Columbia, Discovery, Endeavour,* and *Atlantis*—all became operational; and when many different technologies were thoroughly investigated. A time when numerous developments were put to test in a culmination of past and present learnings to head toward the future and the unexplored.

Two Grumman X-29 aircraft, featuring one of the most unusual configurations in aviation history, were flown on 302 research missions at Edwards. The concepts and technologies the fighter-like X-29 explored from late 1984 to late 1992 include the use of advanced composite materials in aircraft construction, variable-camber wing surfaces, strake flaps, a computerized fly-by-wire flight-control system, close-coupled canard foreplanes, and its unique forward-swept-wing with its thin supercritical airfoil. Powered by one afterburning 16,000lb-thrust General Electric F404-GE-400 turbofan engine, the first of two Grumman X-29 airplanes made its first flight on 14 December 1984. It was piloted by Grumman test pilot Charles A. "Chuck" Sewell. The single-place X-29 has a wingspan of 27ft, a length of 48ft, a height of 14ft, and a gross weight of 17,600lb. With a flight endurance of about 1hr, the airplane had a top speed of 1,120mph (Mach number 1.6) and a maximum operating altitude of 50,000ft. X-29 number one will go to the Air Force Museum at Wright-Patterson AFB in Ohio, and number two will remain at Edwards for permanent display in the AFFTC Museum. *Grumman*

Following its first flight at Edwards on 14 December 1984, the first of two Grumman X-29 Forward Swept Wing (FSW) Advanced Technology Demonstrator aircraft—on 8 June 1988—made its 200th flight. Its pilot, NASA's Rogers E. Smith, flew it to a speed of 830mph (Mach number 1.23) and an altitude of 46,225ft on the record-setting flight. This particular airplane completed a total of 242 flights (178.5 flying hours) during its original flight-test program. Besides the X-29's practical FSW planform, it featured the following technologies: a triple-redundant DFBW flight-control system; a thin SCW section; one-piece, tip-to-tip advanced composite material wing covers; a trailing-edge variable-camber device; close-coupled, variable-incidence canard foreplanes; nose strakes and strake flaps; three-surface pitch-control devices; and relaxed static stability. Both X-29s had a wingspan of 27ft, a length of 48ft, a height of 14ft, and a gross weight of 17,600lb. Initially funded by ARPA, the X-29 FSW aircraft program was managed by the AFMC (Air Force Materiel Command, formerly Systems Command). The number-one X-29 airplane is shown during its record-setting two-hundredth flight. *USAF*

On 22 December 1988, after fifty-nine flights of 144.9 total flying hours, the flight-test activities on the Mission Adaptive Wing (MAW)—flown on the AFTI F-111A airplane—was successfully completed at NASA's DFRF at Edwards. After its first flight on 18 October 1985, the General Dynamics-built, Boeing-modified F-111A was flown by four NASA and six Air Force test pilots during the three-year, two-month MAW flight-test program. For the MAW program, the F-111s variable-sweep wing was modified so that the curvature of the leading and trailing edges could be varied in flight. The airplane then could fly with optimum wing curvature for subsonic, transonic, and supersonic speeds, offering the potential for greater flight efficiency than with a conventional wing. Reductions in air drag from 8 to 20 percent were noted during the tests, as was a 20 percent reduction in wing bending during maneuvers. During the final phase of the flight-test program, the wing system was evaluated in its computerized automatic modes, whereby pilot inputs directed the computer to adjust for optimum wing performance. *Boeing*

Next page
The Lockheed U-2 Reconnaissance Star, in various forms, continues to be evaluated at Edwards. On 17–18 April 1989, a thirty-four-year-old NASA-operated U-2C set sixteen time-to-climb and altitude records in the C-1F weight class (13,227–19,841lb) and in the heavier C-1G (19,841–26,455lb) weight class at Edwards. The eight Class C-1G records set on 18 April are as follows: Altitude Without Payload, 72,720ft; Altitude in Horizontal Flight, 72,720ft; Time-to-Climb to 3,000m (9,840ft), 1min 10sec; Time-to-Climb to 6,000m (19,680ft), 2min 14 sec; Time-to-Climb to 9,000m (29,520ft), 3min 31sec; Time-to-Climb to 15,000m (49,200ft), 8min 10sec; and Time-to-Climb to 20,000m (65,600ft), 19min 41sec (the final record is a new one that had not previously been established). The U-2C used had frequently operated at such altitudes and higher while performing earth-resources missions for the NASA-Ames Research Laboratory, but the records had never been confirmed by the Federation Aeronautique Internationale as world class records. No special modifications to the U-2C (shown) were made for the event, after which it was retired from service and is now displayed at the Robins AFB Museum in Georgia. *Lockheed*

Chapter 5

Past, Present and Future:
Toward the Unexplored

From its undeveloped beginnings in the early 1930s, to its brisk activities of the mid-1990s, and onward toward. . . its various goals for the future, Edwards is the place where multitudes of aerospace related technologies for yesterday, today and tomorrow have been continously recorded in the annals of US history. Yet, with all the host units of the AFFTC, 412th Test Wing (formerly the 6510th Test Wing), dedicated to ground and flying training, accelerated service tests and tactical test on all USAF aircraft; 650th Air Base Wing, whose mission is the support of flight-test operations; US Air Force Test Pilot School, in the business of training experienced pilots, engineers, and navigators to organize, supervise, and conduct flight test to obtain research, development, and evaluation data on

Three thrust-vectoring aircraft at Edwards AFB, each capable of flying at extreme angles of attack, cruise over the Mojave Desert in formation during a March 1994 flight. They are, from top to bottom, the F/A-18 HARV, flown by the DFRF; the Rockwell-Deutsche Aerospace X-31 EFM demonstrator airplane, flown by the X-31 ITO at the DFRF; and the Air Force F-16 MATV/VISTA airplane, flown by the US Air Force at Edwards. All three aircraft are flown on different programs and were developed independently. The NASA F/A-18 HARV is a test-bed to produce aerodynamic data at high angles of attack to validate computer code and wind-tunnel research. The US Navy X-31 EFM is being used to study thrust-vectoring to enhance close-in air-combat maneuvering. And the US Air Force F-16D MATV/VISTA is demonstrating how thrust vectoring can be used on operational aircraft. *NASA*

experimental and prototype aircraft and systems; and, 650th Medical Group, the base hospital—taking most of the credit most of the time for these numerous aerospace advancements for more than fifty years. The major associated unit—NASA, operating the Dryden Flight Research Facility—remains a significant source of ongoing flight-test research with a multitude of various air vehicles.

Dryden Flight Research Facility

The Dryden Flight Research Facility (DFRF) at Edwards is NASA's premier installation for aerospace flight research. It is located between the South and North Base complexes. In addition to carrying out aerospace research, the DFRF also supports the space-shuttle program as a backup landing site and as a facility to test and validate design concepts and systems used in the ongoing development and operation of the orbiter vehicles.

Long before the DFRF was established in the mid 1940s at Edwards, the US Congress created the NACA (National Advisory Committee for Aeronautics) in March 1915: For the supervision and direction of scientific study of the problems of flight, with a view to their practical solution; and to direct and conduct research and experiment in aeronautics. After World War I, NACA built its Langley Memorial Aeronautical Laboratory at Langley Field (now Langley AFB), Virginia, into use. From then on NACA has been the United States' greatest force for aeronautical research and development. Still, NACA did not venture onto the

Powered by three high-bypass 61,500lb-thrust General Electric CF6-80C2 turbofan jet engines, the first McDonnell Douglas MD-11 tri-jet wide-body jetliner made its first flight on 10 January 1990—Long Beach to Edwards AFB. It was piloted by John Miller, chief of flight operations on the MD-11 program and project pilot for the first flight; the copilot was Tom Melody. This particular MD-11 has a wingspan of 169ft 6in, a length of 200ft 10in, a height of 57ft 9in, and a gross weight of 605,500lb. With a maximum cruise speed of 588mph (Mach number 0.87), it can carry up to 405 passengers and has a two-person flight crew. This first MD-11 is shown climbing-out of Edwards after takeoff on yet another Federal Aviation Administration (FAA) certification flight-test. Following 2,000 flight-test hours with five MD-11s, the type was certified by the FAA in the fall of 1990. Note the winglet (extending above and below the wing tip) on the visible tip of the right wing. Winglets, tested by NASA at its Edwards-based DFRF, help reduce drag and thus fuel consumption at best cruise speed and altitude. In the case of the MD-11, best cruise speed was about 590mph (Mach number 0.87) at 43,000ft. *McDonnell Douglas*

The team of Northrop and McDonnell Douglas was selected to produce two YF-23 "Gray Ghost" service-test aircraft for the US Air Force's Advanced Tactical Fighter (ATF) program. The first example (shown) was powered by two augmented (afterburning) 35,000lb-thrust-class Pratt & Whitney YF119-PW-100 turbofan jet engines. With Northrop test pilot Paul Metz at the controls, the first YF-23 made its maiden flight at Edwards on 27 August 1990. The single-place YF-23 has a wingspan of 43ft 6in, a length of 67ft 4in, a height of 13ft 9in, and a gross weight of about 64,000lb. Its proposed main armament, carried within a large internal weapons bay, was four AIM-9 Sidewinders and four AIM-120 Advanced Medium-Range Air-to-Air Missiles (AMRAAMs). Its secondary armament was one 20mm multi-barrel rotary-action cannon. In a hard-fought competition with the Lockheed-Boeing YF-22 ATF contender, the YF-22 prevailed over the YF-23 after fifty flights in a 104-day period. The winner was announced on 23 April 1991. *Northrop*

The first of two service-test Lockheed-Boeing YF-22 Lightning II aircraft was first flown from Palmdale to Edwards AFB on 29 September 1990 with Lockheed test pilot Dave Ferguson at the helm. The first YF-22 was powered by two augmented 35,000lb-thrust-class General Electric YF120-GE-100 turbofan jet engines and has a wingspan of 43ft, a length of 64ft 2in, a height of 17ft 9in, and a gross weight of about 62,000lb. The YF-22 carries four AIM-9 Sidewinders and four AIM-120 AMRAAMs within three internal weapons bays and a 20mm rotary-action multi-barrel cannon. Following the ATF fly-off competition at Edwards, during which the two YF-22s flew seventy-four flights during a ninety-one-day period, it was announced on 23 April 1991 that the YF-22 had won the event. The Lockheed-Boeing F-22 has entered into the Engineering Manufacturing Development (EMD) phase at this writing, and the first pre-production F-22A is scheduled to make its first flight in 1996. The EMD F-22 will be slightly smaller, lighter, and more sophisticated than its YF-22 predecessors. *Lockheed*

Looking like something out of *Star Trek* or *Star Wars* the second of two Northrop-McDonnell Douglas YF-23s plies the skies near Edwards AFB, circa 1990. First flown at Edwards by Northrop test pilot Jim Sandberg on 26 October 1990, YF-23 number two was powered by two augmented 35,000lb-thrust-class General Electric service-test YF120-GE-100 turbofan jet engines. The configuration of the "Gray Ghost" is matchless, featuring pod-like engine air inlets mounted ventrally, trapezoidal-shaped flying surface, fuselage strakes that run horizontally from wing apex to wing apex all the way around the forward fuselage section, and twin large-area all-movable outward-canted ruddervators (combined rudders and elevators) that, due to their outward-cant angle of 45deg, double as horizontal and vertical stabilizers. A feature of the ATF aircraft is supercruise; that is, they can cruise supersonically at speeds up to 1,100mph (Mach number 1.60) without afterburning. *Northrop*

79

Powered by two afterburning 35,000lb-thrust-class service-test Pratt & Whitney YF119-PW-100 turbofan jets, the number-two Lockheed-Boeing YF-22 (shown) made its first flight, from Palmdale to Edwards AFB, on 30 October 1990. It was flown by Lockheed test pilot Tom Morgenfeld. It was this particular airframe and powerplant combination that won the ATF competition on 23 April 1991. The specific reasons that this YF-22 powered by the YF119 engine won have not been made public. Noteworthy is the way the leading-edge apexes of the YF-22's stabilators (combined horizontal stabilizers and elevators) fit into the trailing-edge of the wing. Further, the stabilators are on the same plane as the wings as shown; and they are close-coupled for improved maneuverability and agility during aerial combat. *Lockheed*

northwestern shore of then Muroc Dry Lake until mid-1946 (NACA was renamed NASA on 1 October 1958).

In the summer of 1946 then, after traveling from NACA's Langley Research Center (as it is known today) in Hampton, Virginia, a group of five aeronautical engineers arrived at Muroc to begin preparing for the XS-1 (later X-1) supersonic research flights in a joint NACA-USAAF program. Soon, a facility called the NACA High Speed Flight Station was established.

Since the days of the X-1, the facility has grown in size and significance and is associated with many important milestones in aviation history—supersonic and hypersonic flight, wingless lifting bodies, fly-by-wire flight-control systems, supercritical and forward-swept wings, and the space shuttles.

Among the many aircraft flown by NACA pilots at DFRF in earlier years were:

• Early X-series aircraft: The Bell X-1, Bell X-2, Douglas X-3, Northrop X-4, and Bell X-5. These research air vehicles pioneered flight at and beyond the speed of sound and proved the concepts of swept-back flying surfaces, rocket propulsion, variable-geometry sweep wings, delta-shaped wings (the Convair XF-92A, not a dedicated research plane, but an air vehicle relegated to the investigation of delta-shaped flying surfaces), and semi-tailless aerodynamics.

• The North American X-15A and X-15A-2: This was a rocket-powered air vehicle that extended manned aircraft flight to more than 4,500mph and to altitudes above 350,000ft. It was the first aircraft to use thrusters for pitch, yaw, and roll control on the fringes of space. Flown between 1959 and 1968, it is considered the most productive and successful of any research aircraft to date.

• The North American XB-70A Valkyrie: This prototype of a proposed triple-sonic bomber, flown by NASA between 1967 and 1969, remains the largest and heaviest research airplane ever. Research data from it was and continues to be available for the design of future military and civilian aircraft.

• Lifting Bodies: Five wingless air vehicle designs—the M2-F2, M2-F3, HL-10, X-24A and X-24B—were flown from 1966 to 1975 in a program to obtain data about controllable atmospheric

reentry that contributed to the development of the fleet of US space shuttles that, through 1994, have successfully flown more than sixty times from lift-off to touchdown. An earlier NASA-designed, DFRF-built lightweight lifting body, the M2-F1, pioneered the concept and paved the way for the formal program with the heavier vehicles mentioned above.

Recent Projects

More recent projects led to significant advancements in the design and capabilities of numerous military and civil aircraft.

In the 1970s DFRF modified a former US Navy Vought F-8C Crusader II with an all-electronic flight-control system, and with it, explored the digital fly-by-wire (DFBW) concept used on many of today's military and commercial aircraft.

Another Crusader in the 1970s, an F-8A, was the test-bed for a new airfoil called the supercritical wing (SCW). The F-8A SCW airplane, with its NASA-designed airfoil, proved that aircraft could fly at high subsonic cruise speeds (about 600mph) with lower fuel and power requirements, improving economy. The SCW airfoil—flatter on top and

Next page
Developed under the US Air Force Advanced Technology Bomber (ATB) program, the Northrop B-2A Spirit is the world's first and still only low-observables or stealth heavy bomber aircraft. The flying-wing B-2 has neither vertical nor horizontal tail surfaces. Instead, with the use of a quadruple-redundant DFBW flight-control system coupled to trailing-edge flying surfaces, the B-2 is "tricked" into performing like it has a tail group. Powered by four non-afterburning 19,000lb-thrust-class General Electric F118-GE-100 turbofan engines, the Spirit can carry a bomb load 5,180mi without in-flight refueling and 11,500mi with one in-flight refueling. With its side-by-side weapons bays and rotary weapons launchers, the B-2 can deliver up to twenty nuclear bombs (B61 or B83) and up to eighty 500lb conventional free-fall bombs, precision-guided bombs, or sea mines. The two-place B-2 has a wingspan of 172ft and a gross weight of 400,000lb. The first B-2 arrived at Edwards on 17 July 1989 following its first flight from Air Force Plant 42 at Palmdale. On 17 December 1993, the first operational Spirit was delivered to the Air Combat Command's 509th Bomb Wing at Whiteman AFB, Missouri; it was delivered from Edwards. Shown is the number-one B-2A near Edwards, circa 1990. *Northrop*

First flown at Edwards on 23 May 1989 by NASA's Stephen D. "Steve" Ishmael, the number-two X-29 was largely used to investigate high-angle-of-attack characteristics and the military utility of the FSW planform. Here, during a NASA visual flow test in 1991, tracer smoke flows from tiny ports in the nose of X-29 number two during a study of airflow over the air vehicle at a high angle of attack. Also used during the visual studies were tiny cloth tufts placed on the wings and fuselage, which were photographed to document the flow of air over the various components of the airplane in flight. The final flight on the X-29 program was on 30 September 1991. The program began in late 1984 and employed two Grumman-built X-29 airplanes. The first X-29 validated predictions that the FSW could reduce drag by 20 percent and enhance transonic speed regime (600–800mph, or, Mach number 0.90–1.20) maneuverablity. The second X-29 showed that the FSW concept produced even better-than-expected high-angle-of-attack flight control, flight maneuvering, and flight agility at up to 45deg of angle of attack and still had limited controllability at 60deg. The appendage behind the tail and above the engine exhaust nozzle is a spin-recovery-parachute housing. *NASA*

This head-on worm's-eye view of F-117A number 831 at Edwards clearly shows the types inward-opening weapons bays doors, its extended weapons racks, and a pair of 2,000lb laser-guided bombs (LGBs). First flown on 18 June 1981 by Harold C. "Hal" Farley, Jr., a Lockheed test pilot, the F-117A was secretly evaluated at Tonopah Test Range, Nellis AFB, Nevada, for some seven years before its long-rumored existence was finally verified in November 1988. By then the type had been fully operational for more than five years, since October 1983. Following 49th Fighter Wing's (formerly 37th Tactical Fighter Wing) move to Holloman AFB, New Mexico, from Nellis AFB in mid-1992, the F-117A shown was flown-in to Edwards for continued flight-test and weapons-delivery evaluations. Powered by a pair of non-afterburning 10,800lb-thrust General Electric F404-GE-F1D2 turbofan engines, the stealth fighter has a humble top speed of 560mph (Mach number 0.8). It has wingspan of 43ft 4in, a length of 65ft 11in, a height of 12ft 5in, and a gross weight of 52,500lb. Production of the F-117A, unofficially dubbed "Nighthawk," came to an end in July 1990. At that time, total US Air Force procurement ceased at five full-scale-development planes and fifty-nine production planes. The airplane shown is the forty-seventh production F-117A. *Tony Landis Photo*

more rounded on the bottom than a conventional airfoil, is now employed by a number of military and commercial aircraft.

Other major programs in recent years include:

• The Mission Adaptive Wing: A wing on which leading and trailing edges could be contoured in-flight to form an airfoil best suited for the aircraft's speed, altitude, and maneuvers. The airplane, modified by Boeing, was a General Dynamics F-111A formerly employed in the Transonic Aircraft Technology and the Advanced Fighter Technology Integration (AFTI) programs.

• Oblique Wing: Research flights to evaluate the concept of pivoting an aircraft's wing in flight to reduce drag above and below the speed of sound were carried out with a specially built airplane called the AD-1 (AD meaning Ames-Dryden). Also called the scissor-wing, the oblique wing was in a conventional position (straight-out on either side of the fuselage) for takeoffs and landings, and slanted to up to 60deg during flight.

Today at DFRF

The current major programs at DFRF include:

• Lockheed SR-71A/B Blackbird: Three triple-sonic SR-71s—two As, one B—have been loaned to NASA by the US Air Force and are used at DFRF for aeronautical research that must be conducted at very high speed (Mach number 3.2-plus) and very high altitude (80,000–90,000ft). The data being collected by the SR-71s will help in the continuous development of future high-speed, high-altitude military and civilian aircraft.

• AFTI F-16: The AFTI F-16 program is a joint NASA/US Air Force effort evaluating advanced digital flight controls, automated maneuvering, voice-activated controls, and close-air-support attack systems. More than 600 AFTI flights have been completed at this writing, and the AFTI F-16 research and test results could be applied to future military aircraft.

• X-31: The X-31 International Test Organization (ITO) is, at this writing, located at DFRF, and flight-test operations with the two Rockwell-Deutsche Aerospace X-31 thrust-vectored air vehicles continues. The pair of X-31s are being flown in a program managed by ARPA to demonstrate the value of thrust-vectoring, coupled with an advanced digital-flight-control system, for close-in

air-combat maneuvering at high angles of attack. The information provided by the two air vehicles could be applied to the development of highly-maneuverable next-generation fighter aircraft.

The Future

Planning is underway at DFRF on the flight-test program for the National Aero-Space Plane (NASP) that is expected to be tested at Edwards in the late 1990s and early 2000s. Dryden's Thermostructures Research Facility is also carrying out early structures research on components that may be used to build the NASP. Expected to fly at up to 14,000mph (Mach number 18.4) in the upper atmosphere, the liquid-hydrogen-powered NASP will also have the capability of achieving low earth orbit (an altitude of 100–125mi or 528,000–660,000ft) and still operate from conventional runways. To support the NASP's development, and other potential aircraft using liquid hydrogen fuel, a Liquid Hydrogen Structural Test Facility was built at DFRF to conduct load and thermal static test of structural components used in liquid-hydrogen fuel systems.

Space Shuttles

Among the most visible projects involving the DFRF has been the fleet of space shuttles.

The facility was the site of the space shuttle ALT (Approach and Landing Test) program in 1977. Five times the prototype space shuttle *Enterprise* (OV-101) was used in the ALTs to verify the glide and handling qualities of the air vehicle following its return into the atmosphere from space. During the ALTs, *Enterprise* was carried aloft atop NASA's Boeing 747 transporter and air-launched for a glide-flight back to the lake bed or the main concrete runway at Edwards. These tests went so well that a sixth ALT was canceled, clearing the way for operational shuttle flights. US Air Force Maj. Gen. Joe Engle was commander on the second and fourth ALT flights.

Since the first orbital flight of *Columbia* (OV-102) in April 1981, while Runway 15 at Kennedy Space Center, Florida, was being completed, the majority of landings have been at Edwards. At this writing, if weather permits, all shuttle landings will now be in Florida. But if a shuttle has to land at Edwards, after it is serviced, it is ferried back to the Kennedy Space Center atop NASA's Boeing 747 Shuttle Carrier Aircraft.

Dr. Hugh L. Dryden

The name of the DFRF honors an individual who is a significant part of NACA-NASA history.

Dr. Hugh L. Dryden was an internationally known aeronautical scientist who became a member of NACA in 1931 while working for the Bureau of Standards. In 1946, he was appointed NACA's Director of Aeronautical Research, NACA's highest full-time official at the time. He was responsible for making NACA's High Speed Flight Station a permanent facility in 1947 and was named director of the facility in 1949. When NACA became a new agency under the name of NASA in 1958, Dryden remained as deputy administrator until he passed away on 2 December 1965. The facility at Edwards was named the Dryden Flight Research Facility on 26 March 1975.

Now retired, NASA's F-15 Highly Integrated Digital Electronic Control (HIDEC) airplane—the seventh McDonnell Douglas F-15A Eagle—cruises through airspace near Edwards on a flight out of NASA's DFRF in mid-1990. This Eagle was used to carry out flight research on integrated digital electronic flight- and engine-control systems. The F-15 HIDEC demonstrated improved climb rates, fuel economy, and engine thrust as a result of these new systems. The airplane also tested and evaluated a computerized, self-repairing flight-control system that detects and compensates for damaged flying surfaces. Nearly all the research carried out in the F-15 HIDEC program is applicable to future military and civilian aircraft. The F-15 Short Take Off and Landing/Maneuver Technology Demonstrator (STOL/MTD) airplane shown later in this book has, at this writing, replaced NASA's F-15 HIDEC airplane. *NASA*

Today's DFRF at Edwards is a part of the NASA-Ames Research Center at Naval Air Station Moffett Field, near Mountain View, California.

In concert with the AFFTC at Edwards, the DFRF continues to study the inner and outer limits of aerospace technologies for current and future aircraft.

And indeed, if not for such investigations during Edwards' past and its present, the potential advancements to be made in the future would be for naught. Dr. Jim Young, chief historian at the AFFTC History Office said it best: "If it can happen, it will probably happen at Edwards."

The McDonnell Douglas F/A-18 Hornet High Alpha Research Vehicle (HARV) flown by NASA's DFRF carries out high-angle-of-attack research over Edwards AFB. Its thrust-vectoring system, linked to its two engine's exhaust nozzles, was installed for its high-angle-of-attack research program. The thrust-vectoring system, working in concert with the aircraft's flight-control system, moves a set of three paddles on each engine to redirect thrust for directional control and increased maneuverability and agility at angles of attack at up to 70deg. Data from the NASA F/A-18 HARV program is used to validate computer codes and wind-tunnel results and could lead to design methods providing much improved performance in future fighter aircraft. *NASA*

First flown at Palmdale (some 30mi from Edwards) on 11 October 1990 with Rockwell chief test pilot Ken Dyson under glass, the first of two Rockwell-Deutsche Aerospace X-31 Enhanced Fighter Maneuverability (EFM) demonstrator aircraft is shown near Edwards on 18 September 1992 as it achieves controlled flight at 70deg angle of attack—just one of the aircraft's goals. Later, on 29 April 1993, the number-two X-31 (shown elsewhere) successfully executed a minimum radius, 180deg turn using a post-stall maneuver, flying well beyond the aerodynamic limits of any conventional aircraft. The revolutionary maneuver has been dubbed the "Herbst Maneuver," after Wolfgang Herbst, a German proponent of using post-stall flight in air-to-air combat. The X-31s were to be transferred to the Naval Air Test Center at Patuxent River, Maryland, following their high-angle-of-attack and Herbst Maneuver demonstrations at Edwards. But, after a number of simulated dog fights with F-16s and F/A-18s (which the X-31s won hands down for the most part), it was decided to keep them at Edwards through at least fiscal year 1994. Moreover, after the rudder was locked-out and the flight-control system was told the airplane did not have a vertical tail, the X-31 performed heretofore impossible maneuvers. Afterward, to further investigate its new-found capabilities, its vertical tail was removed! With its reduced drag—no tail, and reduced radar cross section—the X-31s maneuver on at Edwards. *NASA*

First flown at Palmdale on 19 January 1991 with Deutsche Aerospace chief test pilot Dietrich Seeck at the controls, the second of two X-31 EFM demonstrator aircraft is shown during a test hop at Edwards in early 1992. Both X-31s were transferred from Palmdale to Edwards following their respective flight-test activities there (108 flights between them). Designed and constructed as demonstrator aircraft by Rockwell International Corporation's North American Aircraft and Deutsche Aerospace (formerly MBB or Messerschmitt-Bolkow-Blohm), each X-31 is powered by one afterburning 16,000lb-thrust General Electric F404-GE-400 turbofan jet engine. Both X-31s had a wingspan of 23ft 8in, a length of 43ft 3in, a height of 14ft 5in, and a gross weight of 16,100lb. With an altitude capability of more than 40,000ft, the X-31s design speed of 600mph (Mach number 0.90) is more than adequate for its EFM demonstrations. The ITO (International Test Organization), managed by ARPA, conduct the flight-test activities. In addition to ARPA and NASA, the ITO includes the US Navy, the US Air Force, Rockwell International, the Federal Republic of Germany, and Deutsche Aerospace. NASA's DFRF at Edwards was responsible for flight-test operations, aircraft maintenance, and research engineering on the X-31. *NASA*

The second of two General Dynamics F-16XLs sharply banks over a desert community near the DFRF at Edwards, circa 1991, to display its unique "cranked-arrow" delta-wing planform. The aircraft were modified in 1991 to investigate laminar-flow at supersonic speeds in a program designed to help improve the design of future commercial transports and high-performance military aircraft. NASA's F-16XL (formerly an F-16B), has a single-seat F-16XL partner (formerly an F-16A). Originally, the F-16XL aircraft, first flown in July 1982, were in an Air Force competition to find a dedicated dual-role (air-to-air/air-to-ground) all-weather fighter. Its competition, the McDonnell Douglas F-15 Strike Eagle, prevailed and is today's F-15E. *NASA*

This trio of Lockheed SR-71 Blackbird aircraft (two model As, left and right, and one model B, center), loaned to NASA by the Air Force for high-speed, high-altitude research, pose on a ramp at the DFRF at Edwards. These three former reconnaissance aircraft can fly at speeds exceeding 2,000mph (Mach number 3.2) and at altitudes higher than 85,000ft. Their unique operating environment—they are the fastest and highest flying manned aircraft in the world—makes them excellent platforms to carry out research and experiments in a variety of areas such as aerodynamics, thermodynamics, high-speed and high-temperature instrumentation, structures, thermal protection, and sonic boom characterization. Retired from Air Force service, these are only three of six SR-71s still on flying status. Their manufacturer, Lockheed Advanced Development Company (the Skunk Works) likewise retains three SR-71s at its Palmdale facility. *NASA*

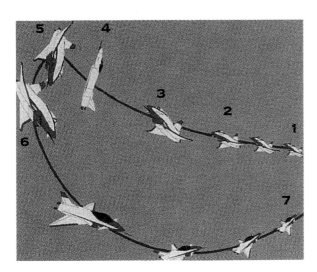

On 29 April 1993, the second of two Rockwell-Deutsche Aerospace X-31 airplanes made aviation history at Edwards when it reached a major flight-test program goal— successfully completing the radical Herbst Maneuver. The maneuver, as shown, is entered at high speed (1), and accomplished following rapid deceleration (2, 3). While approaching a 70deg angle of attack—well beyond conventional aerodynamic limits—the aircraft's unique thrust vectoring ability is used to maintain control (4). Upon achieving an angle of attack of 70deg or more, it then reverses direction 180deg (5, 6) with a turn radius about 80 percent tighter than that of conventional maximum-rate turns (7). This increased agility is a unique air-to-air combat advantage that has allowed the X-31 to meet and defeat such noted fighters as the F-16 and the F/A-18. *Rockwell*

NASA's unmanned, remotely-piloted aircraft, Perseus, flies low over Rogers Dry Lake on its first flight, which took place on 21 December 1993 from the DFRF. Perseus, designed and manufactured by the Aurora Flight Sciences Corporation at Manassas, Virginia, was first towed into the air by a ground vehicle. At an altitude of about 700ft, the air vehicle was released, and its engine turned its tail-mounted propeller to propel the airplane to its desired test altitude. Perseus is optimized to carry scientific payloads to high altitudes to investigate atmospheric conditions. The data it collects will bridge a gap between measurements now gathered from NASA research aircraft and space-based scientific experiments from satellites and space shuttles. *NASA*

On 15 June 1993, after a very successful flight-test evaluation by the Air Force at Edwards AFB, NASA took charge of the F-15 STOL/MTD airplane at the DFRF. The tandem-seat F-15 STOL/MTD is a highly modified McDonnell Douglas F-15B Eagle—in fact, the first B-model produced. The airplane, using a multi-axis thrust-vectoring system, is used as a test-bed for a number of advanced research projects replacing the DFRF's F-15 HIDEC research airplane, shown elsewhere in this book. The DFRF first used the F-15 STOL/MTD airplane in the Advanced Control Technology for Integrated Vehicles (ACTIVE) program to investigate improvements in cruise speeds and trim drag reduction during cruise flights or maneuvers. The first phase of the ACTIVE program (ongoing as this writing) began in late 1993 and concentrates on parameter identification, system optimization, and integration efforts. The F-15 STOL/MTD canard foreplanes are modified F/A-18 Hornet stabilators. *NASA*

93

Conclusion

It is a hot, dry and windy place. But nevermind these three shortcomings, because to the dedicated experimental aircraft aficionados, it is nirvana. That is how it was more than fifty years ago, how it is today, and how it will be tomorrow.

Recently at Edwards, 2 October 1992, the Flight Test Historical Foundation in concert with the Jet Pioneers Association of America, Bell Aerospace Textron, General Electric, and the US Air Force celebrated the fiftieth anniversary of jet flight in America: 1942-1992. The Bell XP-59A Airacomet, powered by two General Electric Model I-A turbojet engines, made three flights on 2 October 1942. Bell test pilot Bob Stanley (deceased) made the first two flights that historic day. The third flight was flown by US Air Force Col. (later Lt. Gen.) Bill Craigie. General Craigie, who passed on in early 1994, along with numerous other Jet Pioneers Association members, attended the day-long celebration that marked the golden anniversary of their respective accomplishments in bringing the jet age to America. Whether they designed, built, or flew this particular airframe and powerplant combination, for them, and for America, it was a day to remember.

More recently, 7–10 September 1994, the US Air Force Test Pilot School held its fiftieth anniversary at Edwards. Members, both from Wright Field in the past and at Edwards, were in attendance for the celebration.

And before you know it it will be 14 October 1997, and another such event will take place at Edwards. For on that date, the fiftieth anniversary of supersonic flight will come about, marking Chuck Yeager's historic flight through the sound barrier and past the speed of sound in the rocket-powered Bell X-1.

Edwards continues to move toward the unexplored. Witness the elegant Northrop B-2, the world's first and only stealth bomber; the McDonnell Douglas C-17, the world's most advanced airlifter; the Rockwell-Deutsche Aerospace X-31, the world's most maneuverable fighter-like airplane; the Lockheed F-117, the world's first and only stealth attack bomber; and the McDonnell Douglas F-15E, the world's best dual-role fighter. And tomorrow with the projected appearance of the proposed NASP, the beat will go on at Edwards. For it too will be extensively tested there.

From the P-59 in the past, to the B-2 in the present and to the NASP in the future, Edwards AFB remains the magic place where aircraft and spacecraft are immortalized or chastised.

Edwards will continue to provide the shape of wings to come.

Bibliography

Books

Angelucci, Enzo, with Bowers, Peter M. *The American Fighter*. New York, NY: Orion Books, 1987.

Bowers, Peter M. *Boeing Aircraft since 1916*. Annapolis, MD: Naval Institute Press, 1989.

Bowers, Peter M. *Curtiss Aircraft 1907– 1947*, Annapolis, MD: Naval Institute Press, 1979.

Francillon, Rene J. *Lockheed Aircraft since 1913*. Annapolis, MD: Naval Institute Press, 1987.

Francillon, Rene J. *McDonnell Douglas Aircraft since 1920*, Vol. I. Annapolis, MD: Naval Institute Press, 1988.

Francillon, Rene J. *McDonnell Douglas Aircraft since 1920*, Vol. II. Annapolis, MD: Naval Institute Press, 1990

Knaack, Marcelle Size. *Post-World War II Bombers 1945–1973*. Washington, D.C.: US Government Printing Office, 1988.

Knaack, Marcelle Size. *Post-World War II Fighters 1945–1973*. Washington D.C.: US Government Printing Office, 1985.

LeVier, Tony with Guenther, John. *Pilot*. New York, NY: Bantam Books, 1990.

Miller, Jay. *The X-Planes: X-1 to X-31*. New York, NY: Orion Books, 1988.

Pace, Steve. *Vought's F-8 Crusader*. Simi Valley, CA: Ginter Books, 1988.

Pace, Steve. *North American XB-70 Valkyrie*. Blue Ridge Summit, PA: TAB Books, 1990.

Pace Steve. *X-fighters: USAF Prototype and Service Test Jet Fighters XP-59A to YF-23A*. Osceola, WI: Motorbooks International, 1991.

Pace, Steve. *F-117A Stealth Fighter*. Blue Ridge Summit, PA: McGraw-Hill, 1992.

Pace, Steve: *Lockheed F-104 Starfighter*. Osceola, WI: Motorbooks International, 1992.

Pace, Steve. *Lockheed Skunk Works*. Osceola, WI: Motorbooks International, 1992.

Pace, Steve. *Edwards AFB Experimental Flight Test Center*. Osceola, WI: Motorbooks International, 1994.

Pace, Steve. *North American B-25 Mitchell*. Osceola, WI: Motorbooks International, 1994.

Pelletier, A.J. *Bell Aircraft since 1935*. Annapolis, MD: Naval Institute Press, 1992.

Stoff, Joshua. *The Thunder Factory*. Osceola, WI: Motorbooks International, 1990.

Wagner, Ray. *American Combat Planes*. Garden City, NY: Doubleday and Company, Inc., 1982.

Wegg, John. *General Dynamics Aircraft and their Predecessors*. Annapolis, MD: Naval Institute Press, 1990.

Periodical Articles

Young, James O. "The Golden Age at Muroc-Edwards." *Journal of the West*, Vol 30, No. 1 (January 1991).

Military Histories

History of the Air Force flight Test Center: Bi-annual AFFTC History Office Volumes, various sections, 1954–1972.

Young, James O. *Supersonic Symposium: The Men of Mach 1*. Air Force Systems Command, 1990.

Index